EXPLORATIONS INTO THE BEING AND DOING OF COACHING

A collection of voices, insights and wisdom from Austin coaches

ISBN-978-0-578-30970-5

Printed in the United States of America

This book is dedicated to our Austin community of professional coaches, past, present and future, in celebration of 25 years of collective knowledge.

CONTENTS

Introduction

Experience vs imagination has been a shared professional trek of substance for the coaches contributing chapters to this book. We all at one point had to imagine what becoming a coach, then actually doing coaching with clients, would turn out to be. Fortunately for each of us, this has become a fulfilling life endeavor.

As the chapters came in, we, as editors, began to note how seamlessly they started to divide into two camps: the "being" a coach and the "doing" of the actual coach-work with clients be they individuals, teams or other groups, often organizational groups. As we reviewed the chapters, we realized each coach had gone beyond their training which varied broadly and trans-formed their version of coaching simply through doing the work, by coaching. They also discovered the creativity within their platform for "in the moment" work that could build client trust. This seemed to happen regardless of the type of coaching they offered - or clients they gained whether it be business or life oriented. Sometimes the work became in tandem with a bit of both, possibly in transition or career expansion or changes brought forward by the Covid-19 changes or related family ones.

Within these pages you will find processes and practices our authors found leading in their own growth. You will also find how clients can morph goals and relationships both personal and professional. They bring all of themselves into their work with their coach. Though this is not intentional, what these chapters have revealed is how distinctly being a coach, plus having a coach, shares coaching benefits. Families often report having their family member in coaching seems to change other aspects of their lives. Several of us have even had the spouses or close relatives of a client say, "Please stay in their life. We can ALL tell when you have met - and that is a VERY good thing!" What we suspect is happening is that we are all growing into more fully human, humane and kind people.

Recognizing what is timely and specifically relevant for you, as a reader, will become obvious as you make your way through these chapters. You will realize how important knowing yourself beyond the ordinary is. Many of the coach authors capitalized on capabilities in which they already excelled and assisted them in bridging into this profession especially when those capabilities paired well with their freshly gained coaching skills. In the mindfulness chapter, the coach-author references how coaching can be less about destination or a pre-set goal and more about learning how whole and complete the client (or team of clients) may already be when being fully present to and with each other.

A piece of coaching includes confronting a client and then rejoicing together when the confrontation led to the client getting out of their own way. In a different instance, we find a coach who is not sure of what to do next with a new client, then offering a presence that created a client-condition to receive exactly what was most needed during that session. Another coach tells us of cultivating growth experiments that allow for the skills of empathy and assertiveness to develop and work together. Several of the coach-authors reference the immense value of self-reflection plus feedback and co-discussion with and from colleagues - or via supervisory, trusted others or a strategically selected mastermind group.

Another took this opportunity to speak of becoming self-aware, extraordinarily self- aware, as one needs to gain insight into the following questions by doing structure introspection such as: Who am I? Who do I want to be? How do I fit into the world? And often it is a world that is changing. How do others see me in my professional role when I may be blind to this myself? As coaches, one of our tasks and privileges is to support clients with structure to help them see themselves through the eyes of others which can lead to active insight such as what type of leader they are being in contrast to their own level of understanding of what that has been. All can catalyze into fresh levels of understanding what a specific desired change may become often in situations where differences in power exist and may not be spoken of openly.

The coach-authors in this book demystify how coaches and our readers are already using emotional intelligence and effectively so. The presence of emotional intelligence in our lives provides growth steps and ideas to build upon almost by the very nature of it. In the current times, being aware of emotional intelligence informs our experience such as when we are happy or not and how we perceive and choose appropriate behaviors.

One chapter delves into how coaching approaches can nurture loving-kindness toward self and others. By the completion of that chapter, we hope you will have genuine interest in acknowledging, accepting, understanding and using feelings in a constructive way that possibly eluded you previously.

The chapter on personality assessments provides a comprehensive overview and set of specifics on how personal characterics can impact decision making, thinking, perceiving and feeling. Again notice how much is pointing to catalyzing change, being a useful part of change and managing self. This leads us right into how as a coach one of the unique ways we can assist clients can be in supporting how they have integrated their character strengths into having dependable awareness of who they are now and who they may want to become in the future. Sound familiar? Yes, it is clearly in one of the territories of our themes. Fitting right within this trend we find resiliency and just in time some may think. Resilience as represented here is in bouncing back from change - good change as well as change we may perceive initially as quite bad, serious change, as serious as death or substantial loss of good health or a much appreciated job. Keep reading – there are positives ahead.

Laced within all this is the obvious: the power of questions, such as, what is our purpose in asking a client a question? To avoid telling? Not giving advice? Understanding or avoiding misinterpretation? Experimenting with the process? The author-coach of this chapter unwraps communication components and mental models.

Then as myth and metaphor often become the means by which we inform and instruct ourselves according to Joseph Campbell, can the concept of "the story we tell ourselves" be leveraged by the coach for the client- and put to work. Could this wise dose of wisdom unfold for us in the form of a one-thousand pound horse as a sentient, non-judgmental reflector? Yes, and here's a whole new version of it. This horse and his heartful coach bring us a true story of a courageous young boy who changed how he was dealing with the feared future and, together with his parents, re-invented how he stepped into his future with confidence. For those of us who have also instinctively loved horses, prepare to now learn why.

Overall, fourteen coach colleagues built the mosaic this book turned out to be. Post-training, specifically coach-trained, each of us blossomed into delivering coaching quite differently. All of us report growing during that process in differing but continuing ways. What emerged for us in "how to's," "what if's" and "when-then's" has been fascinating. The editors enjoyed being a part of the process and its discoveries. Our offering here, by intention provides a direct look into the life of a "working coach" and to some extent, the benefits fostered by being in this field. Some mention what they take back into their life and the significant people in their lives and others speak of value-adds gifted by being part of a healthy coach-community.

By now you notice patterns within a few of the highlights we bring forward. The relevance and power of listening – and especially in being fully heard – will be one. Others range from client-related commonalities in stories; business tips around being in this business; reflection recommendations; and even a bit of speculation; along with journeys into truth-telling (privately or shared); the startling appreciation which can be profound when listened to deeply, followed by complete sharing of silence. Comfortably shared silence together seems to be quite rare in our current culture for many. The language of considerate minds is particularly welcomed at this time. Coaches tend to use the language of the personal and the personalized naturally. This book can open and initiate views into the experience coaching can deliver without lapsing into any of the "he said, she said" quotes or second-hand hearsay.

While most of these pieces are what some of us "do" as coaches working within client-settings, the emphasis throughout is personalized whether individually or with teams or in group work organizationally. If we move readily between "I" and "we" and "you" in our narration, it makes our many types of exchanges and work settings more universal. Sometimes that allows the self-aspect to come into greater focus; sometimes it is because much about what you will find within really is quite transferable.

Woven into this collection we were gratified to find how topics voluntarily contributed as subject matter worked naturally together. The voice of the book soars between conversational to a supportive, evidence-based informational, slightly academic, to warmly informal. It gave us a sense of spaciousness representative of what we most often find in our industry - a collaborative spirit. A sense develops that there is a coach for everyone who wants one and there is enough interest in coaching to go around. We hope, as a reader, you find a combination of chapters in length, depth, wholeness and writing style as joyful as we have found in weaving this book together.

We know one of our collective pleasures in compiling this book for an organization's 25th anniversary has been sharing and completing the collaboration. The rich co-learning gleaned in the chapters we have shared is something to treasure especially during an otherwise isolating pandemic. Thanks are definitely in order all around both for starting and completing it at such a remarkable time in our history.

- Sherry Lowry, Michelle Hefner, Susan Corbin

THE BEING OF
COACHING

KNOW YOURSELF FIRST

by Sherry Lowry, MCC

What I am advocating is a journey – a journey of repeated reflection on what matters. I learned early on engaging within this coaching field – and in coaching itself – there was something to look forward to as I was delivering results with clients over and over. It has never become "work" for me. Coaching is good for me. I've even found during times of personal challenge, maintaining some degree of "working" is grounding and provides structure that adds to my overall balance. It serves as a means of refueling as well as a gratifying challenge. This is an opportunity in contrast to a job and I've gratefully accepted the fact the industry allows us such flexibility.

It is a part of the way I recharge and simultaneously build new skills and refine my coaching expertise and perform in my role whether that be as a coach, as a team player or as a supportive encourager or follower. It also helped me discover and understand what I never wanted to do again even if others thought that was a strength of mine. If it was, it was not a satisfying one. Recognizing what is timely for you will be part of your reading journey here.

A profound benefit from knowing myself better has come through reflecting on what being a part of the coaching industry itself has returned to me. That, plus my work with individual clients, teams and companies changed who I was and who I began to become. I'd been a business owner multiple times including as a solo entrepreneur and a founder of what became a 20,000-client non-profit. But the type of changes being a coach catalyzed went beyond what I anticipated in committing to work primarily with owners and founders of other client-based businesses. Pursuing this coaching career has worked out well for my professional life and has created cherished, long lasting relationships along the way that are still vibrant today two decades later.

What follows I've found true and reportedly so, do those working as I do as a business coach, or if they are a wellness coach, a wealth coach, a resilience coach, a collaboration, grief, mediation or any other variety of coach particular clients seek. I believe if you seriously embrace the process of becoming a coach, you will naturally be changing; you will be growing; and your own personal and professional evolution can become part of the work of coaching. It helps if some of the other capabilities you bring in with you readily transfer to bridge and pair with your coaching skills. This is why I state endeavoring to "know yourself first" at every level and step will reap return. Developing as a coach will tend to bring out the best in many of us. It may be because if you are in this business, you are going to keep showing up as yourself which is encouraged, encouraged with colleagues and with working partners. As you expand and deepen your own training – all this is transferable into how you are with your clients.

A hope is to get to the heart of the truth about what we actually want to glean in providing and reading this book and in our coaching life. I know in building my first coaching business, I liked it so much I soon wanted to learn to diversify, morph and build onto it as it gained a life of its own. Part of what worked so well for me was as our culture and my life-stage changed, my business could evolve in response. Of course, my "frame of mind" had to broaden and deepen as my own learning about myself, the field and the client-work itself did. In that process I formed some critical beliefs I could count on about myself - as to what I would stay interested in and stick to as my own family's developmental leaps occurred. One critical ob-servation helped shape the type of client-base I developed. It is: <u>I've never had a client who needed a stronger weakness</u>. Clients and I tend to work together instead on deepening, strengthen-ing and customizing what they can identify is already working they can transfer or by focusing on what could work better. I also found helping clients figure out what's enough enables them to rise to their challenges while accomplishing their goals without burning them out in the process. We also discovered for most, making a deep change commitment happens in a heartbeat; the challenge becomes maintaining their attention on every posi-tive change, small or large, once created so they can build upon it.

I learned I had natural springboards to harness and leverage. What became easy was often what I was already prepared to step into by background or experience, not what I had to learn about from scratch. Those activities or series of actions seemed to take off and succeed more readily and they drew others in collaboratively. Awareness of safety nets grew out of paying at-tention to inklings, hunches and intuitive grasps of understand-ings that often paid off. Studying those patterns also taught me what I was wise to move more toward or away from in my own process. Coaches can benefit from listening to their internal sig-nals. People come into them by learning through what seems coincidental but then with experience, patterns noted begin to provide context as to who and what to trust.

I do not want to leave out what may be our most significant gift to both clients and others be they family, soul mates or best friends. This is a multi-faceted approach to listening I will go into more detail with later. Clarity is a natural benefit of such full-spectrum listening. Be watchful to welcome the new and emerging which often can follow.

Discovering what is or is not a good client and project type combo for you often surfaces in tracking what already is naturally succeeding. One example I quickly figured out was overloading on coaching within my "sweet spot" (working with founders and owners) was not sufficient diversification in the longer term. I was wiser to cultivate clients at different levels and stages of business operation and size including corporate hires of high potential and working across multiples of generations. What emerged I came to identify as my **High Road** that both kept me in highest integrity but also positioned me to be working on my growing edge and the unknown rather than "settling in" and becoming over-comfortable with the known. It helped me build a more differentiated client base which was better for me developmentally. I anticipate you have, or will have, your own **High Road** – one you design and build-out with what you choose to do over and over that keeps you also in highest integrity. Sticking to my High Road gave me agility I lost by succumbing to a sideroad of the shiny that was interesting but was not of substance. It is amazing how easily we forget what we know is best for us and in some cases, what we actually are even in the business of holding for others when they forget for themselves.

If we know both what we consistently want more of and less of in our future, there is much richness and flexibility available. We can design and build a business with potential to change as we change, as the culture changes and as the economy asks us to innovate and adapt. This is all why "knowing yourself first" deserves a primary focus as you craft a new coaching career, create a pivot within the one you have, or are operating independently or within a coaching firm or a company that wants your capabilities. This applies as well if you are considering becoming a coaching client.

Equally important for me became identifying my priorities in founding my own coaching company and attuning to differing developmental stages – my own and those of companies and clients. Periodic planned reflection on what I continued to value most in my own life consistently let me honor my needs for flexibility and choice. This became true not just in my monthly and annual endeavors but also in my literal daily and weekly calendar organization. A hope I hold is that your reading of this book sprinkles small cues to help shorten your learning curves and enhance your work satisfaction.

Let me provide a concrete example in my own training to become a coach I tried out but could not keep implementing. Many training programs recommend a new coach or a coach-in-training do demonstration or "Demo Coaching" wherein you offer people a no-charge session of your coaching approach for the sake of business development. I had to learn more people may want you to "coach" them than would be wise to "coach." Possibly a potential client was hoping a "shortcut" through gaining a trained coach would be helpful in contrast to getting more communication or other skill-building themselves. Or, they didn't want to go into therapy or whatever other type of self-improvement they sought in working on themselves. Possibly they did not yet realize a coach will not do the work for them though one can make entry into the new and fresh goal attainment go easier and even faster.

I tried it and learned fast I had to quit demonstration coaching – not because I didn't enjoy it; not because it did not go well enough but I discovered there were a lot of people I <u>could</u> match up with – but who could be much better served by someone else, someone more in step with them than I felt I was. So, for me, it was a bit of learning the hard way to figure out a better avenue to have a simpler exploratory, real conversation with a potential client instead. If any coaching took place within that exchange, they may experience that beneficially - but I had not "promised" a sampling of coaching in advance. I found this approach gives the exchange more real working room to become a contribution to them. It helps define the value of coaching to themself - and I've done no "coaching convincing" in the process. That actually became my purpose – not to enroll another client but to work with each to create take-away value just through the conversational exchange. At the same time, I've gotten to know a person better. If they become a potential future client then or in the future, we'll together determine the type of preliminary interview we may want to conduct prior to that happening.

Another area I found key to knowing myself well was life-stage related. Rather than retire years back, I refashioned my coaching business to allow me to glean as great a gratification in supporting other talented coaches at all levels as in coaching more and more new clients myself. That led me beyond forming my coaching company into also simultaneously serving as a coaching credentials assessor for those acquiring their own certification. I separately established myself as a "Mentor Coach" for those already credentialed and needing to renew. All this delivered another learning: considering your time sacred. If you also get industry-engaged, you may be wise to know what keeps you on your own growing edge professionally. But doing some of it is a wonderful means of more thorough learning of coaching rudiments.

You can see all this requires self-reflection on a repeat basis. That did not come naturally to me. I had a fortunate stumble into it more out of frustration in seeking my own clarity. At different points, I knew I was ready for a change and wanted to carry some things forward but not everything. So I began with a spreadsheet that turned out to be in the details.

inadequate by the first hour. I marched to the store instead and got some butcher paper. With that I created a facsimile of a spreadsheet but on paper. I drew columns on this and strung it all over the wall which helped me stay in the bigger picture rather than tangled   In the first column was: **What Can I NOT Keep Myself From Doing?** What am I going to do over and over and enjoy no matter what? That became my priority #1 to do more of in the future. I made a list of all the different things you can't keep me from doing. One turned out to be connecting people. It gives me pure pleasure. Another was continuous learning. I am a therapist by background. One of the reasons I loved that industry but ultimately decided to leave the field and the very hard-earned credentials was because I was too restricted in connecting people I felt could benefit from meeting each other. (Ethically, as a therapist you just can't go about individually introducing clients to each other, socially or for other personalized reasons.) The first column on that spreadsheet was all about what I wanted to increase the "doing of" or had a real avid taste for in my future.

The second spreadsheet column was **Never Again!!** Like all of us, I learned some things I knew I was done with but had fortunately documented in writing. How did I know? Good at such or not, if it energetically drained me, it was sent into the **Never Again** column. For example, while I may be good with detail, I don't love the process of recording specific details as a data-person might. So I made a commitment to have the accounting aspect of my business externally contracted in a way I trusted from almost the very beginning. I fortunately was able to contract with an accountant colleague who admired what I was doing in my business. We made an agreement that lasted three full years. She would set up and maintain all my accounting, financial data management and IRS reporting for me and I would help her with launching a new segment of her business. She sought transitioning to work with psychologists, other holistic professionals as her new niche as opposed to law firms. She not only succeeded but also gained the skill of yoga so she could teach for fun at retreats.

(As to barter, the best way we found to do that was to regularly co-exchange our monthly fees. So while money did change hands and was on both our "books," we essentially felt we had been mutually investing equally. She remained my accountant for two decades after our three-year barter completed.) What can you outsource with glee? Find out.

The third column was if I wasn't going to do something myself and it was an essential to my business, I still had to take responsibility for getting that covered so who was to do such? That third column became **Hire It, Contract It or Put On Hold.** I had those three columns. If I did not fill that last one quickly, I had to be patient, hang it on a hook and wait. Almost always someone would spontaneously show up who wanted to do just that. Plain luck played a role in that which was okay with me.

That was the basic underpinning of what became my business structure. That's the same one I'm still periodically reinventing over two decades later. Along the way, I learned I periodically still need a fourth column: it is always temporary but deserves attention. It is what I am willing to do, could do, capable of doing well myself, I may be asked to do often by others, but don't really enjoy it so I learned to make sure it always has a short-term timeframe connected to it. That's burnout territory for me - doing something repetitively out of necessity so it also has to come with a replacement plan as well as a duration time frame. It can exist but only to be enacted with boundaries. Those become the messages I send.

A side benefit became a commitment to my own well-being and that of my business. This gradually gave me the confidence and the willingness to negotiate a bit which carried over into: **How Did I Truly Want To Schedule**? Having been a therapist in the past meant I once worked by appointment. In that structure, I billed by the hour or appointment, dollars traded for time. I knew I wanted to schedule more flexibly. Ultimately, I'll provide my comfortable dollar range, they choose within that, then together we estimate a time-range duration for the work. We want that to include how they process and organize for lasting change and to feel it a realistic one to accomplish their own end of "the work." Most importantly, we both become clear what our work is to be and that it is a working partnership. Our outcomes are dependent upon this. We can mutually renegotiate on this timing as we need to and as we agree to revamp and modify our agreement accordingly. Sometimes the work may simplify and we may adjust the fiscals or our frequency in response. Often before those initial sessions complete, we are ready to revise our agreement and continue our work in an "on call" fashion or until the client wants to do otherwise or I do. The mutuality of this - plus the evolvement over time of our agreement- gives it a vibrant life.

Now and from the beginning of this career, in making my appointments, I am the one who typically names the dates I am available. Almost always I am able to give the client their choice of which days and time of day we work together. It's an easy question: does a morning or afternoon work best for them? Or alternatively, I may ask for their own first TWO options and I will fit within one of those if I can. I still can control my schedule. (None of this may be a value to an experienced coach but if you are new to thinking about your scheduling and billing structures, these possibilities may be a consideration.) Something else I learned is my clients do take our work seriously and do not want to be late or miss an appointment so I assume if they do have to reschedule, they have good reason to do so. They give me the same benefit should I ever need to change an appointment even on short notice. In short, we have no penalty needed around scheduling. There is a mutual trust and good intention around an assumed arrangement.

This brings me to one of my most invaluable learnings as a coach about the business of coaching when something does become less than a good fit for me: Knowing how to say, "No" – and to say no gracefully and comfortably. In my case, "No" is a complete sentence. Sometimes, most often I am more comfortable with "No, but this is interesting, just not now. Will you ask me again in three months when my work schedule (or special project or…) has shifted a bit?" What I've learned is people who are serious about whatever they asked me to get involved with WILL come back in a timeframe of possibility or they will not.

Some people ask me to share alternative "No" techniques. I don't really consider this a technique but I learned to use how I am put together energetically as a part of being true to myself. I tend to have naturally high energy so before I even consciously know why, my energy will perk up and rise and actually be my guide both with people and ideas - as to mutual resonance. It is something I can read - a little like a temperature sign in my own territory. My energy rises and falls around conversations as well as ideas or with certain people and it may fall or decrease with others. I pay attention to all this. It tells me to wait and think more about something or to make a decision pretty quickly or not. I bet you have something like this also. As a coach, I often help bring a client's attention to what their own energy is telling them. We've all heard: "The body never lies." I believe that and believe I benefit from paying attention to it. Neuroscience is helpfully explaining so much of this to us now quite literally. I'm grateful for it.

How can we apply this capacity most bodies naturally possess to our decisions to work with a client or not when that opportunity presents? I mentioned I may take an energetic "read" at the onset of (say) an introduction. It's not an option - it's more of simply noticing I have a "felt sense" at that moment. If that "felt sense" changes abruptly or simply feels energetically neutral, that's additional information and I note it. A lot of times in earlier days I made referrals because of this when a potential client did not feel exactly right for me. Other times a colleague as a perfect fit may come directly to mind based on what the potential client shared. I've never regretted making referrals when this happens - though I may not know until much later why I thought it good timing and good for the referred person to do so.

Discovering what type of listener I wanted to be was a milestone and one of my most gratifying discoveries. I wanted to be a 360 degree listener: As the science supports, active listening, accompanied by unconditional positive regard, supports clients better than most anything else in making productive changes. That form of listening is part of our being fully present with and for the Client. It involves **listening to**, **listening for**, and **listening with**. Listening fully is our most extraordinary skill we can gift to another whether it be a client, a friend or a significant other. A big surprise to me early on as a coach was to experience a client who was once a school district superintendent who had done a lot of lifetime listening himself. We were in a restaurant for an exploratory meeting – eating salad I recall. He got very quiet. I looked up to see big tears streaming down his face accompanied by a glowing smile. He was deeply touched with feeling so completely respected and heard and was showing it. That was my first public experience of how readily a simple conversation can become sacred to another. What was so key to him was how he was able to completely finish his expression to me of why he wanted a coach, without interruption, without question and how it felt having that simply received. In his previous executive world apparently that type of personal spaciousness within a meeting to complete an expression fully was rare.

This is also what some clients mean when they say, "My coach just "gets me, every time, all the time." It creates a strong sense of trust and of traveling in stride together - often into their unknown. That type of trust and rapport is irreplaceable.

How does this happen? By not speaking up as soon as a client completes a thought, by allowing a client to fully finish what else may be there, we furnish the chance for them to hear themselves and to feel the impact of their own thoughts. Often those are thoughts they've never before stated aloud. Then by taking the time ourselves to ponder what they shared, often the client will spontaneously elaborate and create on the spot what may be unexpectedly unfolding for them for the first time ever as to where they want to take their life or business. (Note: Our own comfort with silence when together is part of what is key so get comfortable with it early-on.) Everyday life does not often give this opportunity. Coaching often has these moments when the body and mind may breath and notice just in being in connection like this, what they may have been missing and what life is clearly inviting them into next.

When we as coaches, take the time to **listen to, listen for**, and **listen with,** we also often hear what may be missing or wanting to also be present. I often hear during such times what was <u>not</u>

said but that was intended. An important function of the coach may be to name that, ask about it or support the client in identifying it (naming it) for themselves. It is also in such moments we as coaches can be listening for values, purpose, commitment, even vision as any one of these may surface to be newly recognized by the client - and welcomed. The coach can also become the temporary "holder" of the client's "bigger picture" while they tend to fleshing out the details of it and begin the process of bringing such to reality in their life, their business or their future.

A major difference in the way a coach is trained to listen is we are not listening for "solution" or a verbal break when it becomes our turn to talk or to add our own brilliant idea for the client. Instead, we are listening for the client's aspirations, their discoveries, their strengths that they may have in abundance and take for granted and do not even know may be extraordinary - and sometimes even rare. A lot of people do not know these things about themselves. They have taken them for granted. The discovery and validation can be very encouraging. This type of intuitive listening with consideration of their whole self and with heart builds resonance and the experience of genuine communication and caring, a sense of companioning and this is confidence building that lasts and without encumbrance. While we often ask clients to take risks and explore new behaviors, in this case it may be the coach's willingness, with no answers at the ready, to go into the completely unknown future with the client when it seems timely.

I am also often listening for what I consider The Big 5 with the client. This is a set of concepts (but as her Big 4) Lynn McIntyre Coffey generated long ago with her "Listen – Mirror – Path – Floodlight – Method" she fully documented in her book, *Simply Coaching--For Your Highest and Best,* (c)2018 Lynn

McIntyre Coffey, Highest and Best Publishing, Inc. She and I have often marveled together over how processes and the watchful eye of a coach can become solid gold for the client's own benefit when they are goal setting. Clients themselves often are not overtly aware of what they already have abundance within (or in overload) or what they may be obviously in deficit around. This may not be clear to them given they are so close to their own situation. Highly talented or perfectionistic clients who are both ultra–productive and overworked can also be under-resourced clients. This may show up when together you start to examine their circumstances in each of these areas:

1. Focus

2. Mindset/Attitude

3. Skills & Capabilities

4. Habits, Practices and Patterns (present or missing or hit-or-miss)

5. Energy - and their available level to share or lack of such

An in-depth exploration around these very areas with their coach helps evidence for a client why they are sailing through a situation easily or trying their best without the expected success they relish but are not reaping results. Such examination can point them to needs they did not realize they had plus the resource of natural abundance they have available to further harness. Personally knowing all this in each area is clearly clarifying and clarity is often exactly what a client seeks.

You can see how this type of knowledge can play into a good strategy's bottom line if what can be identified is already their existent competitive advantage in a challenge. Good strategy provides you a way through or a timely, cogent response to a challenge. It lets you build a bridge between purpose and action, between desire and feasible outcome. Here are some qualities of a good strategy:

- faces "the problem" squarely
- can be stated and defined
- it is NOT fuzzy
- provides a filter and forces choice
- is not fluff or idealistic chest-beating
- is not a "goal" or pie-in-the-sky objective without evidence
- is based on your competitive advantage via your existing resources and capabilities

What creates confusion around strategy is the difficulty for people to choose. If we refuse to choose that too often means we also refuse to focus and it's hard to hit what we aim for without focus.

As I bring this Chapter to completion, I also want to acknowledge several more colleagues. In San Antonio, Texas, there is Jennifer Navarrete, creator of Brewing Media; and in the Houston area there is Sonya Ware, founder of Blue Beagle Consulting and Ware Shift Happens. Both independently gave me very good pieces of examples of what effective business as we know it almost always includes especially when building an alliance or a collaboration.

This business concept started to emerge for me in conversation with Jennifer who said, "My business relationships that really build into something significant start in the **head**, that means there is a logical common sense connection of why I am drawn to that person or that project, that capability they have or their distinctive way of being. That very quickly involves **heart** because I tend to care more about what it is they are presenting or bringing to the table. When it is in a business frame, a **wallet**, it may be a good investment for me to spend more time with that person or learn more about what it is they know or how they go about being in their life. That cultivates **relationships**." Then Sonya Ware and I spoke more about this conceptually to then transfer it into a frame. Key elements were how dependably together all this touched on aspects of connection via **head, heart, wallet, or relationship**. Sometimes they overlap, or one becomes more central but the combination together builds trusting rapport. Again you can see how valuable having an extended community is. Jennifer is part of mine, just as is Sonya, as is Lynn McIntyre Coffey in Colorado. I think of them as three of my own four-quadrant resources of professional friends. They often see and point out in commentary – or their own – work nuances I take for granted myself. I trust the judgment of each. Having such trusted colleagues is a blessing of being in this field.

You may find your own similar type of **four quadrant** reflection a useful one to run through when doing self-determination of what you want more of in your business, what you want less of, what you want to start, and what you want to stop. This seems to be a useful mantra to me. Most of us know these things and they serve as a good place to conclude and reinforce why Know Yourself First is a really good place to begin when thinking about the coaching life or having a coach in your life. Thank you for your interest in this.

Questions To Consider:

- If you are considering becoming or acquiring a coach, why now for you rather than last year or next year?

- What is it now that you want more of in your life or business, what you want less of, what you want to start, and what do you want to stop?

Bio

Seven times entrepreneur, Sherry Lowry is a coach strategist & mentoring collaborator. Her primary clients are owners, company high potentials and a small collective of evolving coaches.

A primary interest is catalyzing the talented become leaders-of-self first. She finds once self-managed & self-led, the whole room stops to listen when they speak. Their own best ideas become actively pursued and received as they elevate others.

A Houston native, she moved to Austin, Texas as soon as she could in 2002. Her businesses have ranged from solo entrepreneur to founding a 501@3 that her staff of eight and two hundred volunteers help grew to 20,000 clients

A committed gardener who loves the kitchen, and finds sharing the results pure pleasure. These days discovering she has a creative nonfiction voice, and one that still surprises her, has led her to a deep dip into the study of literary craft, including personal essays and short stories.

More detail can be found if wanted at https://sherrylowry.com .

THE MINDFUL COACH: STEP INTO YOUR COACHING GREATNESS

By Shelley Pernot, PCC

I'll never forget those first coaching sessions when I started my solo practice. There I was, bright eyed and bushy tailed, fresh out of coaching school, jumping for joy while I excitedly waved my newly printed ACC certificate high in the air so eager to help my first few paying customers navigate the murky waters of life's journey to enhanced fulfillment, peace and contentment. So basically, no pressure on myself. I was confident that I was the one who could show my clients the way. I would lead them to the elusive light of nirvanic awareness with my newfound coaching prowess! Now if only I could remember the right coaching questions to ask...

That first year was painful. There I was dutifully writing down every word my clients said paranoid I would miss a key detail that would enable me to unlock the secret formula to their success. Half the time I missed most of what they were saying as I was trying to formulate the perfect powerful question in my mind that would stop them in their tracks. After each session I'd spend hours replaying it in my mind not hesitating to beat myself about where I had failed as a coach. Was that question powerful enough? Oh crap, that was a closed ended question! Was the goal of the session clear enough? Oh crap, I bet it wasn't!

More often than not, I punished myself for my client's failure to achieve the oh so coveted epiphany moment we so crave as coaches. At times, I found myself wondering if I had just spent a rather large wad of cash on something I would never be good at.

Sometimes I'd get nervous in a session especially if the client was more of a big fish so to speak. What if I ask a stupid question? What if I don't understand their business well enough? What if I piss them off and I get the sack? What if they walk away from this session thinking I'm some sort of woo woo, new age beatnik that uses words like energy and mindfulness – things that busy, successful people have no time for?

I hate to admit this but it's true, if you haven't guessed it by now: I'm a recovering perfection junkie. And like many recovering perfection junkies, I from time to time have an overactive mind that can become more of a foe than a friend. And even after all these years of building my coaching practice and feeling like I somewhat now know what I'm doing...it still happens from time to time. I lose the plot, my mind hijacks me, and I'm off to the races.

If you've been coaching for a little while or a long time, chances are you've heard about mindfulness. Perhaps you have a steady meditation or yoga practice. Perhaps you even encourage your clients to adopt such practices for themselves or have found novel ways to integrate it into your sessions for your clients' wellbeing. After all, mindfulness is the modern-day holy grail as it's been linked to benefits such as work life balance, emotional intelligence, resilience, stress management and more. But the focus of this chapter is on you as a coach and how mindfulness can help you be an even more fantastic one. So what is mindfulness really, particularly as it applies to the art and science of coaching? Why is it so important to work towards becoming a mindful coach? And finally, how the heck do you do it?

Let's start this discussion with my definition of mindfulness.

Mindfulness: The practice of focusing awareness on the present moment non-judgmentally.

Practice

I use the word practice very deliberately in this definition for the express purpose of letting us perfection junkies (you know who you are) off the hook. Practice makes better. There is no perfect allowed anymore in my new world. I don't care if you're a coach that's been seeing clients for 50 years or you've trekked up to the Himalayas to levitate in a cave with a bunch of Tibetan monks. No one has mastered this. No one maintains perfect focus in the present moment 100% of the time and lives in a peaceful state of nirvanic bliss, free from the craziness of their inner saboteur. Okay, maybe Buddha. He was kind of cool.

Case in point, just the other day, there I was in yoga class doing my not so best in the confines of the sweaty hot room to mimic my graceful swan of an instructor in warrior three perilously balancing my long lanky six-foot frame on the tippy toes of just one foot when my mind was hooked by something way more exciting - my Trader Joe's shopping list. Asian dumplings, olive oil, ranch water...if you get nothing else from this chapter, try the Thai Asian dumplings at Trader Joe's. You won't be disappointed. But I digress...

Back to the topic at hand, if you don't believe me with respect to our innate human difficulty to focus, according to Harvard Business Review, 50% of the time we are mentally off task. That means 50% of the people reading this chapter didn't take in what this sentence said (you know who you are!).

Present moment

When I think about mindfulness, I often think about a dog track. Stay with me for a moment; I promise this is going somewhere.

Focus on the track itself. You watch the handlers parade the dogs around the track and load them into their starting cages. 3....2....1, and they're off! Yippee!!!!!

Focus on the dogs now. They're chasing a small mechanical rabbit thingee around the track. Now, think about what happens. Do the dogs ever get the rabbit even after they cross the finish line? Well, of course not you're thinking. That's why they run. And you are right. The dogs run and they run and they run. The next day they wake up and do it all over again. And they never catch the rabbit.

And that is precisely how most of us live our lives. We never really are where we currently are. We spend our time in the past, ruminating about things that went wrong or we spend all our time in the future, a sure-fire recipe for anxiety. Chances are you see it very clearly in your clients, the wise and sage-like coach that you are. They pride themselves on their busyness and fill their lives with activities and tasks to avoid being present with the oh so unsavory aspects of themselves – their pains, their fears, their emotions. You hear them saying, "When X happens, then I'll be happy." Or, "Once I've finished Y, then I won't have to worry."

Let's say they even get said X or Y. The happiness is fleeting because they're now fixated on a new want or have found a new worry to occupy their time. This is why I've often mused that coaching is less about the destination and more about helping clients learn they are whole, complete and perfect even in this seemingly imperfect present moment.

We coaches fall victim to the curse of the mechanical rabbit too no matter how enlightened we may be--more clients, a better website, a new video series, a bigger, more prestigious coaching contract, a new corporate client. We fixate on these things and forget to be present. We forget our true value lies not in our accomplishments but in the gift of our mindful presence.

Imagine you're really there for your clients. You're not thinking about the next client you've got that day, the next proposal you still need to write, the next bill that needs to be paid, how the last session didn't go as well as you wanted it to. You're listening deeply, intently, to every word they say. You're the king or queen of focus. You're an ace at "holding space" as we coaches love to say. And we could all use help improving in this area especially considering as each year passes our collective attention span reduces exponentially. I think we're now hovering around the attention level of a gnat. I blame the smartphone.

So what is a poor, distracted coach to do? Well, there are plenty of things. We could start with the obvious things, things like starting a yoga practice or a meditation practice. I promise no flexibility required for yoga. But there are also specific, in the moment things too, and oh how I do love to be specific.

Deep Breathing Before a Session

I once heard someone talk about square box breathing. It's one of these mindfulness practices often touted at meditation retreats that sounds super fancy – you inhale for 4 counts of breath, hold your breath for 4 counts, exhale for 4 counts, and then hold your breath again for 4 counts. In your mind imagine a perfectly square box. 4, 4, 4 and 4. Voila! Inner peace here I come!

Well, it didn't work for me. I kept wondering if I was doing it right. And then at one point near about induced myself into a panic attack when I was convinced the cadence was causing my heart to stop. Go figure.

Now that I'm older and mellower, I sometimes spend a few minutes before each coaching session doing some simplified deep breathing, just in and out. I've ditched the box – in for a count of 4, out for a count of 4. Any number will do really. I've also had clients who are super keyed up and distracted with nervous energy during a session suddenly stop what they are saying, close their eyes and I count them through the breathing for a minute or two. Works like a charm.

For you kinesthetic folks out there, a quick body scan before a session can also help to ground oneself, as well as focus in on any tension you've been holding onto. It's not mindfulness perfection but hey, it works.

Minimize Distractions

If you're tactical like me, there are loads of ways to minimize distractions. Put your cell phone in a drawer – even if it's on silent. You'll see the text message pop up and the lure will be oh too strong to resist. I used to teach a course for years on effective planning and the number one thing that helped people stay focused throughout the day wasn't a fancy tool; it was simply turning off email notifications – you know, those annoying little things that pop up at the bottom of the screen to say you have a new message. Sometimes they even make a nifty little sound like the ting of a slot machine. These things are mind crack, and they've been invented to trap you. Don't be fooled, you have no self-control.

Even better yet - close out of your email completely before you start a coaching session so you won't even be tempted to take a little peep. These are simple things to do but common sense doesn't necessarily equate to common practice and the longer we've been coaching the more we fool ourselves into thinking "I got this," and often bad habits will accumulate over time. And while we're on the topic of notifications this goes for all of them: instant messaging, slack, skype, whatever the latest and greatest app is you have installed now. Particularly now that coaching is more virtual than ever before, your laptop and phone are fraught with temptations.

This is my favorite part of my definition which I especially included for my fellow perfection junkie friends who often suffer from imposter syndrome. Take a few moments and think about the following questions:

- What would my coaching look like if I didn't judge myself?
- How would my coaching improve if I didn't judge my clients?
- What if I didn't have to prove myself?

Talk about powerful questions!

I mentioned earlier that everyone from time to time forgets their true value, falls victim to the curse of the mechanical rabbit and blindly enters the chase. If you think long and hard about why that might be, it often boils down to judgement. Particularly self judgement or in other words, "I'm not _____ enough." You can fill in the blank with any creative word you choose. Smart, experienced, competent, knowledgeable, hardworking, perfect are a few that come to mind based on my journey to date.

I ask myself the above three questions regularly now. I even have them written out on a post it note and pinned to my monitor, lest they fade into the dusty recesses of my memory.

The difference in my coaching has been profound. I listen more intently as I've stopped worrying about whether I'm doing a good job. I ask questions from a genuine lens of curiosity without making assumptions as to what my clients' answers will be. I challenge my clients more often and am not afraid to push them beyond their comfort zones. I've even fired myself from engagements because I realized I wasn't the right fit for the client or they weren't in a position to do the work. And I didn't take it personally.

This is why mindfulness is so powerful. When we remove judgement out of the equation, it opens the door to possibility. The less we judge, the more present and mindful we are. We perfection junkies love to shame and blame ourselves. But when we fall into that trap, it takes the focus off the client and what is ultimately best for them.

I'll never forget this one client I had, we'll call her Valerie.

Session after session, there she was in my office, complaining about her life, her husband, her career. I dreaded my sessions with her. I couldn't shift her thinking no matter how much I acknowledged and validated her pain. No question, no matter how brilliantly worded, could break open those pesky assumptions and inferences she was desperately clinging to. I blamed myself. My mind was full of self judgement and before each session I beat myself up:

"Well Shelley, obviously if you were a better coach, she'd be making more progress by now."

One day, a few minutes before she arrived for our session, I closed my eyes, took a couple of deep breaths and gave myself permission to say or do anything that would serve her. No matter how bold. No matter how rooted in tough love it would be.

No matter what her reaction would be. I repeated over and over to myself out loud, "Whatever I say will be right. Whatever I say will be exactly the thing she needs to hear. Whatever I do will be perfect in this moment."

I found myself challenging her for the first time ever in that session. I asked her to think about what she wanted, particularly whether she really wanted to do this work. I told her I was tired as her coach. That I was ready to step away from the engagement. That perhaps I couldn't help her and that was okay.

The next session after that was profound. Within those two weeks, she'd thought more about how she was getting in her own way than at any other time in her life. She showed up willing to do the work.

Ironically, what it took for me to help break that open for her was letting go of seeking perfection as a coach. Funny how these things work.

Now, this lovely little anecdote wasn't just for fun. It also begs the million-dollar question, "How do you get in your way as a coach?" Or in other words, how might judgement be hijacking you out of the present moment and limiting your capacity to move your client forward?

I encourage you, oh wise sage-like coach, to spend some time thinking about this one. No matter how adept you are in your coaching prowess, you're still human, and we all let our self-doubts and inadequacies get the better of us from time to time.

So I hoped you enjoyed this brief parlay into the magical

world of mindfulness. And just in case you weren't paying perfect attention throughout this entire chapter (you know who you are!), I've summarized the key points below for your review.

Chapter Summary

- Mindfulness is the practice of focusing your awareness on the present moment non-judgmentally.

- Don't worry about being mindful 100% of the time. It's a practice, and practice makes better!

- Practice tips such as minimizing distractions – close your email, turn off notifications, hide your cell phone before each session. We all develop bad habits over time no matter how long we've been coaching!

- A couple of deep breaths or a quick body scan before a session can make a huge difference in the quality of your coaching.

- Think about how you judge your coaching and get in your own way. When we fall into this trap, it takes the focus off the client and ultimately what is best for them.

- Remember the 4 Mindful Coaching Questions:

  - What would my coaching look like if I didn't judge myself?

  - How would my coaching improve if I didn't judge my clients?

  - What if I didn't have to prove myself?

  - How do I get in my way as a coach?

Bio

Shelley Pernot is an ICF certified career and leadership coach, and the owner of <u>True North Coaching,</u> a firm dedicated to helping folks discover their talents and grow their careers. She learned the importance of tuning into passion the hard way; for years she blindly followed a career path that didn't suit her and eventually came to the conclusion life is just way too short.

Shelley is passionate about the topic of mindfulness, so much so that she has dubbed herself the Irreverent Guru of Mindfulness and integrates the practices into everything she does. Her mission is to bring mindfulness into the mainstream, as experience has convinced her it is the foundation to living a joyful life and the one quality that separates a great from good leader. Sher regularly facilitates mindfulness and leadership development workshops and has worked with organizations such as Dell, Baker Hughes, Shell, Amgen and the University of Texas.

Prior to launching True North, she was Global Capability Manager for Leadership Development at BP. She is a certified yoga teacher, a hiker who enjoys being outside as much as possible and the founder of the 1 in 6 Sistership, a fun tribe for childfree women 35 and up.

TO MAINTAIN PRESENCE WITH THE CLIENT

We Must First Maintain Presence With Our Value

By Joshua Boyer, ACC

"I have frequently seen people become neurotic when they content themselves with the inadequate or wrong answers to the questions of life. They seek position, marriage, reputation, outward success or money, and remain unhappy and neurotic even when they have attained what they were seeking. Such people are usually contained within too narrow a spiritual horizon. Their life has not sufficient content, sufficient meaning. If they are able to develop into more spacious personalities, the neurosis generally disappears." — Carl Jung

From the beginning of my coaching journey I have struggled with the concept of *value* and knowing what I am worth. Of course I mean this in terms of market value but what I am getting at is something much deeper that I think keeps us awake at night far more often than the question of what hourly rate our coaching is worth. I am talking about doubting our intrinsic value - a value based entirely on who we are and not at all on what we do. We received this value long before we could do anything for anybody.

I don't remember the day I was born. I do, however, vividly remember the moment each of my four daughters were born and the emotional and physical sensations that overwhelmed me.

I was wrecked.

Every time.

I could not put into adequate words just how incredible and significant I knew they were. I could not explain how or why I immediately loved them so much. There was a newfound depth of love and devotion in my heart that was spiritually birthed in me as I watched them being born.

They were instantly so incredibly valuable to me.

From the moment we are born, we all have value that we don't have to prove to anybody or earn from anybody. Our value is not determined by our behavior, performance, success or achievement. We cannot increase our value, decrease our value, or ever lose it entirely. It does not change depending on our race, religion, nationality, gender, socio-economic status or anything else. We just have it.

And yet we spend our entire lives working hard to earn the things we already have.

How tragic.

Value is deceptive, isn't it?

The majority of us attach our value to what we do - our work, our services, our achievements. But even when the moment of completion or achievement happens, we still feel an emptiness. Thus, after our great achievement, we are no more conscious of or connected to our value than when we first began our quest. The euphoric moment we envisioned where we finally feel fulfilled by all our accomplishments fails miserably to deliver on its promises and we suddenly realize the grinding journey toward knowing and experiencing our value isn't over. The quest continues and the end is still somewhere off in the distant future.

In that moment, we either finally choose to believe we are already valuable or succumb once again to the temptation that we can somehow earn our value through what we do.

Or how we coach.

Or *who* we coach.

Or *how many* we coach.

Is this resonating with you? If so, you are not alone. I once spent weeks crafting the language of my purpose, coaching niche, ideal client, and writing copy for my website, social media posts, ads, and brochures and in one single moment of seeing some other coach's website, threw it all away and started over.

On another occasion, I spent a few days designing and re-designing the coaching services and trainings I could offer, mixed and matched different hourly rates and service packages to engineer the perfect "lucrative coaching business," went to bed proud of my hard work only to wake up the next day and hate everything about it.

I have had countless nights asking myself, "Does anyone else see the incredible benefits of coaching and what I am uniquely offering?"

All of those experiences have ironically taken place even while coaching clients through their challenges, problems and "neurosis."

I have been the blind leading the blind.

And yet, despite knowing that it is impossible to impart to others what you don't first possess for yourself, I still get tripped up and lose sight of what matters most.

The most powerful and effective thing we could ever offer our clients is the version of ourselves that is maintaining a presence with our intrinsic value. Coaching from that place, we more easily maintain presence with the client and therefore create the conditions necessary for the client to receive exactly what they need from the coaching session. When you believe you have value and that you could not do anything to earn, increase or lose your value, you show up differently for the client. You're not afraid of delivering a bad experience. You're not worried about asking the perfect questions. You will know how to be present and you'll know what to ask because you have nothing to lose.

We can only achieve that when we know our value and therefore coach instead of coaching to earn or achieve or prove our value.

So, how do you do that? I'll briefly share what has worked for me and how I incorporate it into my coaching practice though I also believe every coach has to develop a personal strategy that works for them.

Years ago I learned an ancient form of meditation called, "the renewing of the mind." It is practiced in the Christian faith and can be found described in the Bible in the book of Romans chapter 2. It is a simple meditation of replacing old thoughts of shame, guilt, fear, insecurities or powerlessness with new thoughts that are anchored to things that are eternally true about us and about God.

The same practice that years ago led me to freedom in my personal life has become the starting block to all my successful coaching engagements. I incorporate it as a five to ten minute meditative ritual before I am in front of clients. It is brief but powerful. The continual practice of renewing my mind on the truth and reconnecting with my intrinsic value enables me to better maintain presence with the client because my mind and heart have been decluttered. I am free to focus on the client's story instead of self-sabotaging my efforts with a distorted view of reality which is precisely what viewing myself or my coaching as invaluable is: a distortion of the truth.

I'll leave you with this: you are valuable just as you are. There is nothing you can do to increase your value. It is certainly important to increase your professionalism and your skills as a coach. These things matter, too. But they will always pale in comparison to the greatest thing you could ever offer your clients which is just simply you. Your 'market value' may increase to impressive amounts but that will eventually fade away and be forgotten. Your intrinsic value, on the other hand, is eternal, remembered and inherited by the generations that will come after you.

So stop doubting yourself and maintain presence with your intrinsic value. I bet you'll see an increase in your effectiveness maintaining presence with your clients.

Reflections:

- When do you find it most difficult to maintain presence with the client?

- What do you believe is the root issue for you?

- How well are you maintaining a mental, spiritual, and emotional presence with YOUR own personal value?

- What impact would it have on your clients if you could more consistently coach from a belief in your value?

- What truth statement do you need to renew your mind

with today?

Bio

Joshua Boyer is a world traveler and people explorer, raising four extraordinary daughters (and one naughty dog) alongside his beautiful wife. He will be the first to tell you that he is a much better coach than a writer but is also the type of person whose most difficult challenge in life is saying no to a challenge or fun idea. He currently resides in Round Rock, Texas and is a senior trainer and executive coach for a consulting firm helping companies create the conditions for their people to do the best work of their lives. You can find him on LinkedIn @joshuakboyer

COACHING LESSONS

By Susan D. Corbin, PhD, ACC

During one of my first coaching sessions with a graduate student, she explained that she was having trouble figuring out a problem with her research method.

"Do you have any advice?" she asked. I felt my stomach sink. I had no idea what to tell her. It was the kind of problem that had driven me out of the research world.

I paused a few seconds wondering what the heck to say and these magic words came out of my mouth. "What do you think?" I said. The graduate student also paused and then began to innumerate several possible solutions.

In my best coaching voice I asked, "Which of those solutions seems to be the most helpful?" With that she began to discuss the pros and cons of the thoughts she had about her problem. I was thrilled.

Later I realized that I didn't have to know the answer to her problems. I just needed to ask her the right questions for her to figure out what her own solution was. Boy, what a load off of my shoulders that was! I didn't need to know the answers! What

I really needed to know was how to ask the right questions to elicit her thoughts. Here are three ways that you as a coach can help your clients come up with their own solutions. None of these ways is something I invented. They are just techniques I have picked up along the way and use.

1. Listen

2. Pause

3. Ask a question

First, listen carefully to the client. You must have your mind in the present moment. You cannot be thinking of what to have for dinner and then what you need to pick up at the grocery store before you can make the dish you chose. Thinking about the argument you had with your significant other while "listening" to the client does a disservice to both of you. Sometimes taking a five-minute break before talking to a client and doing some deep breathing can ground you in the moment. This allows you to be present for each person who talks to you.

Listen with your ears. Pay attention to tone of voice and cadence of speech. Is the client speaking quickly? Is she excited about what she is saying or does the fast speech seem to indicate that she is fearful? Is she speaking slowly and deliberately as if she is unsure of what she is saying? Does that mean that she's not sure what the problem is or is she fearful about what this problem means to her and her life?

Listen with your eyes and watch her body. Did she walk in and fall into the chair? Is her back curved over and she's staring at the floor when she talks about the problem? Can she barely sit still in the chair due to what seems to be anxiety over the issue? If you are on the phone or a video conference, body cues are harder to pick up and you may have to rely on verbal hints to how the client is feeling.

Listen with your body. Yes, sometimes you will sense subtle things about how a client is feeling without knowing how you know. That's okay. You don't need to know how you know. You just need to pay attention to what your intuition is telling you might be happening within the client.

If you pick up on these cues as you are listening, ask the client if your interpretation of their signals is correct. In the above situation, I said to the client, "It seemed when you came in that you were sad about where you had found yourself in your research. Now you seem much more excited about discovering that you did have some ideas about what to do. Is that the case?"

"No, I think I was more anxious about it at first, rather than sad. And yes I do feel excited about it now. I had not realized that until you mentioned it," she said. No sweeter words to a coach's ears than for a client to acknowledge that the coach had picked up on something the client had not realized yet.

Next, pause. Give the client time to consider what she has just asked you. Give yourself time to consider what she asked. Silence can be an important coaching technique. In the U.S., waiting about 2-3 seconds before giving an answer can help the client feel that you considered her question before answering. Pausing that long can give you the opportunity to decide what question you want to ask next.

However, a pause can be detrimental. Waiting more than four seconds can cause the client to wonder if you heard or are upset with what she said. Using long pauses is one way the negotiators use to get the "other guy" to talk more. The long pause can make some people uncomfortable enough to start talking to fill the silence. Using this technique, the negotiator is hoping the "other guy" will let something slip about what points they are willing to negotiate.

Finally, make an observation, ask for a clarification or ask a "What do you want to do?" question. You've been listening and watching as the client tells you her story. You can comment on what you've heard and seen. I gave an example of a question to confirm an observation above. Did you interpret what you saw correctly?

Ask for clarification. You've heard her tell you the story of her problem. Did you understand all of it correctly? Were there any parts of it that were not clear to you? Even if you are pretty sure you understand what she said, it never hurts to clarify. Ask.

"I heard you say you have two possible ways to go after this data. Is that correct?" I asked my client.

"Well actually there are three ways I could do this but I think only two of them are feasible given the time I have to collect the data," she said.

If you believe that you understand the emotions around the problem and you truly understand the problem, now is the time you can ask that wonderful question: "What do you think you should do?"

Believe it or not, most clients will have an answer. Do not

give in to the desire to make her more comfortable. Give her time and space. Remember what I said about silence. Now is the time to use it to elicit more words from your client. She knows the answer whether she knows it immediately or eventually. She'll figure it out with your listening and questions.

I didn't know all of this the first time I coached a graduate student. I was just thrilled that my asking her what she thought she could do about her issue worked. I realized that I didn't have to know all the answers just like my coaching instructors had told me. Of course I didn't really believe it until I tried it. Since then I've realized the rest of what I've told you here.

Go and coach. You do not need to know the answers. Trust that your client does. Your job is to empower people to see where they are and to know that they know more than they think they do.

Bio

Susan D. Corbin worked at the University of Texas in student support for fifteen years. In her role as Graduate Coordinator, she coached graduate students finishing their doctoral and master's degrees. Since retiring, her coaching practice specializes in helping graduate students finish their graduate programs. A native Texan born in Kermit, TX and raised in Houston, she lives in Austin, TX with her husband of many years and their long-haired dachs-hund, Sadi. In her spare time, she's reading, writing, or playing computer games. Learn more about Susan on her website at **www.corbindissertationcoaching.com.**

IMPROVING YOUR INFLUENCE:

THE INTERPLAY OF EMPATHY AND ASSERTIVENESS

By Kelley Russell-Duvarney, MA, PCC and Marilyn Orr, PCC

Image: Google Creative Commons

<u>Who We Are and Why This Matters</u>

As professional coaches we believe we should always be asking ourselves powerful questions that will allow us to lend greater clarity to those we coach. When Marilyn and I were co-presiding over ICF-Greater Austin's chapter board several years ago, it wasn't uncommon for board members to remark about the differences in our leadership styles. I was certainly more direct or assertive whereas Marilyn often led with connection and affective empathy which resulted in a dynamic duo but was our use of empathy and assertiveness as skewed as others' perceived or were we operating as we intended?

What surprised us both upon further reflection was that we had each been individually working on improving these two social-emotional skills for much of our adult lives and we could easily see the far-reaching benefits we had gained from further development. When well-developed, empathy and assertiveness support us in connecting more deeply and vulnerably with others. We both agreed that after years of intentional improvement we could be more fully available to others, especially during times of need, without abandoning ourselves, our values or our beliefs. In addition, with empathy and assertiveness more fully developed and more consistently expressed we could more easily detect when underdeveloped empathy or assertiveness were preventing our coaching clients from making progress towards their most important goals.

In another twist of fate, Marilyn and I realized we were both certified by Multi-Health Systems, Inc. to deliver their EQ-i 2.0 emotional intelligence assessment and Marilyn has since become a certified trainer. A few years ago, we began serving as coaches on the same coaching contract for a local university that used the EQ-i 2.0 to provide coaching to student leaders. Our interest in the interplay of empathy and assertiveness deepened and we were curious about the ways in which these two important social-emotional skills supported our student-clients' individual goals as well as their leadership development. Interestingly, our work with student leaders has provided us with great insight into the challenges of some of our executive clients who continue to struggle with the interplay of empathy and assertiveness in their own leadership roles.

Fortunately for me, Marilyn's background in Psychology continues to prompt us to consider the individual factors that inform our social-emotional expressions which include factors related to personality and attachment theory. Whereas my background in Sociology causes us both to be more mindful about the external influences of institutions whether the institution is our own family, our workplace or our nation. In this chapter we will share with you some of the insights we have had in our own exploration into the ways in which individual and social conditions shape our expressions of empathy and assertiveness and suggest ways for you to consider further development.

Although Marilyn has provided the reader with a comprehensive view of emotional intelligence in another chapter in this book; however, we would be remiss not to include definitions and to say a bit about how empathy and assertiveness fit into Multi-Health Systems, Inc. EQ-i 2.0 assessment that informs our own understanding.

According to the research literature, cognitive empathy represents our ability to accurately identify another person's thoughts and feelings while affective or emotional empathy is our ability to appropriately respond. Most of us have a sense of what empathy looks and feels like but most people who attend our webinars are often surprised by the true definitions. Assertiveness is our ability to openly communicate our individual feelings, thoughts and beliefs and when appropriate, defend our personal rights and values in a non-offensive manner. Empathy and assertiveness are just two of the fifteen components identified and measured by the EQ-i 2.0 emotional intelligence assessment which is based on the mixed model of emotional intelligence appropriately named the Bar-On Model, developed by Reuven Bar-On in 1997.

You may want to pause at this point to re-read the definitions above since we realize first-hand that few of us are operating with an accurate mental representation of either term or their associated behaviors. During our first webinar on the topic of developing empathy and assertiveness for better influence in the workplace, it was an eye-opener for us both when our female physician participants casually described empathy as 'sugar coating the truth' and assertiveness as a 'male trait'. We began to wonder how these important social-emotional skills had become so maligned and misunderstood and if in fact these misrepresentations informed our resultant behaviors?

Our Premise

In an ideal world each of us would have equally well-developed empathy and assertiveness. Please note that in our conceptual model, well-developed empathy and assertiveness are represented at the 0 in the middle of the continuum rather than at either end. When we overly rely on assertiveness to influence others, we're likely to be viewed as aggressive and when we underutilize assertiveness, we're most likely to be perceived as passive. Likewise, when we rely too much on empathy, we tend towards rescuing behavior and when we fail to lead with empathy we overlook and potentially negate the thoughts and feelings of others. These extreme expressions occur towards either end of the continuum and we believe accurately represents when empathy and assertiveness are underdeveloped or underutilized. As you look at these two separate continuums, please consider the following concepts:

1. My ability to consistently use each skill independently and jointly affects how I show-up in my relationship with others and therefore how I am experienced.

2. Where my empathy and assertiveness are located on

the individual continuums impacts how I will experience you and how you will experience me.

3. Differences between these two skill levels will exaggerate the experience we have of either when they are underdeveloped. When both are developed well and complement each other, they operate to my own individual benefit and to the benefit of my relationships with others.

Assertiveness Continuum:		
Passive	Assertive	Aggressive
-5	0	+5
Empathy Continuum:		
Uncaring	Empathetic	Enmeshed/Savior
-5	0	+5

Figure 1

Pause for a moment to imagine someone very high in assertiveness but low in empathy. There would be an exaggerated effect on how I experience them, perhaps in this case, I may experience them as quite dominant. The same would be true for someone high in empathy but low in assertiveness. This person may appear to be overly caring but lacking a strong sense of self. Now imagine a person who can express both empathy and assertiveness well. They are more nimble, able to use these skills interchangeably and together to accurately respond to what the situation requires. Simply put, they can be there for others without losing themselves in the process.

In our profession of coaching, I have certainly worked with a fair number of coaches who lean hard in one direction or the other and feel certain that their leaning represents the best way to coach. Truly, there are times when we are doing our job well that our clients will perceive our assertiveness through our use of direct communication or observation and may feel uncomfortable or even upset with us. Equally important is the need to intentionally activate our empathy in order to read and respond appropriately to the needs of our clients. We admit that affirmation and acknowledgement are powerful skills to use with our clients but not to the exclusion of our other coaching competencies. In all cases, rescuing our clients under the guise of empathy is counter to our professional stance in partnering with them to reach their fullest potential.

Marilyn

As a child my Mom called me "too sensitive". What I did with that skill of being sensitive (did you catch the reframe?) was very different from what Kelley did. My observations were of my Dad's power to dictate what kind of a day the rest of us would be having gauged by if, and how, his rage happened to take over that day.

My ability to read and connect to how others were feeling was born in self-preservation. I adopted the 'good girl' stance. Being sweet, playing dumb, and never giving others (Dad especially) a reason to be angry at me was paramount. This translated into two things. First, I figured out what activities 'made' Dad feel better about himself and then I would work those in. I clearly remember asking Dad to show me how the furnace worked. Dad felt better, noticeably to me as a little girl, when he could be the authority and be teaching. This magical thinking led me to many years of overusing empathy to my own peril and truly in ways that limited growth possibilities for those I was closest to.

The second thing that this self-preservation stance translated into was a turning off and muting of my beliefs, opinions, preferences and emotions. I was in my mid-twenties when a fellow counseling student, a dear friend, started challenging me about sitting on my anger. She saw anger in me before I could even recognize it was there.

This all contributed to me wanting to be a nurse from the age of 3 until I was 17 applying for college. I didn't get in so did a 'year' of Psychology which turned into a BS in Psychology and later an MA in Counseling. My life goals revolved around wanting to help others heal.

One giant wake-up call happened for me in my early twenties, during my undergraduate studies in Toronto, Canada. I had a friend who was living with out-of-control Borderline Personality Disorder. During an escalating episode she was making violent threats and would show up at my apartment door (she unfortunately lived in the same high-rise building). It triggered a breakdown for me.

A couple of very big realizations happened for me during that very scary and painful time.

1) The vast majority of my relationships were extremely slanted. I was the one trying to help, listen, serve, rescue. Very few of my friendships were healthy and balanced. I wasn't. I led with empathy very much at the expense of myself, very much to the exclusion of assertiveness.

2) One of the relationships I had considered to be healthy ended up helping me with the second realization. Many people and systems wanted me to stay the way I was. Others in

our friendship circle did not think that setting more assertive boundaries was kind. I was pressured to stay open to this spiraling friend. The systems we are in, family units, etc. often have vested interest in us not changing.

As I hope I made clear in the narrative above, when we choose to grow in either assertiveness or empathy or change the interplay between these two skills we do so in our existing systems of friends, family, community and colleagues. These systems exert pressure on us and our clients, often in one direction more than another. At some point in every new coaching engagement, it is important that we take the time to share with our client that behavior change is difficult for both the person choosing to change and for those around them. It is equally important to recognize when the system is working against our progress and sometimes when it may be necessary to exit all together.

Kelley

As a fairly sensitive child it was often hard for me to separate my own feelings from what others were feeling and experiencing. And as a child raised in a home with addiction, the inconsistencies present in my home setting amplified my feelings even further. When I consider that empathy is influenced by both nurture and nature, it is clear to me now that my emotional empathy was often running on overdrive while my perspective-taking remained severely underdeveloped. Fortunately for me I was given the opportunity to explore these inconsistencies in my mid-twenties after connecting with my first and possibly most important mentor.

As for assertiveness, I recall a very early realization that the men I knew were less apt to be penalized than the women I knew for asserting their opinions, beliefs and viewpoints which sometimes included overt displays of dominance. I remember testing the limits of my own assertiveness at home, at school, at church and in and around my community relentlessly and my 'antics' were often ignored or penalized. The assertive behaviors I attempted to model were performed by my older brothers every day of my life and my perseverance worked against me for many years until I was better able to predict the expected balance of empathy to assertiveness for girls in a variety of settings.

In time I began to more accurately thread the *gendered* needle of my expressions by leading with empathy and keeping assertiveness in the background, always alert for the spaces where my own thoughts and opinions could be openly shared. For quite some time though, I vacillated quite a bit between extreme expressions of empathy and assertiveness, rarely performing either very well and often to my own detriment. However, my early, overdeveloped sense of self-awareness helped guide me, along with the support of a trusted mentor, towards developing healthy expressions of both empathy and assertiveness that eventually allowed me to reach many of my goals.

Our Executive Clients' World

Recently in Kelley's work with leaders of organizations it has been very interesting to notice a trend towards companies demanding and expecting more empathy from their leaders. On the surface this sounds amazing! What could go wrong with more empathy, right!?!

With an accurate understanding of empathy we would be in pretty safe territory. If we encourage healthy assertiveness along with it, we would be in even safer territory. What is happening though in some companies is that empathy is being operation-alized in ways that negate accountability. In an effort to be more *understanding* about the demands on any employee's life, letting go of requirements all together around deadlines, and respect-ful workplace behaviors and appropriate communications with direct supervisors is becoming a new norm (e.g. taking time off without asking, etc.).

When we take a complete view of people's lives and consider work culture, family culture, religious culture, childhood, race and gender we definitely need to take a supportive approach with our clients' growth in strategic and sensitive ways. Some growth steps can have big ripples in the systems in which they live and work. For example, when clients start in a new company discrepancies quickly become apparent and this is a time when either the client or the company first notices and can be a time when coaching is seen as helpful.

What is the solution? It is not a simple matter of just devel-oping one of these skills. It is to pause and consider how they are being expressed in their new organization. It is slowing down to assess the client's own personal development levels on each of these social-emotional skills. Then, it is creating growth ex-periments that allow for these two skills to develop and work together.

Marilyn and I would like to wrap-up with a case study that brings together the ideas we have been discussing in this chap-ter and end with resources.

A Take-2™ Case Study (Fictitious)

Jamie has thrived in a number of companies and is excellent technically in the world of IT, specifically networking applications. Recently Jamie started working as the network manager in a new company, a telecommunications company that is also located in a different part of the country. The cultural differences are dramatic and the relational tools that worked really well for Jamie in a previous role are now backfiring and resulting in tough conversations involving HR.

Individual influences - Jamie is very practiced at getting things done and most naturally leads with assertiveness. Let's say Jamie is the quintessential pragmatist. This has been rewarded both personally and professionally for four decades.

Social Influences - Jamie's assertive behavior was rewarded with promotions and excellent reviews for many years. The IT field in general has a lot of people who think that direct, factual communication is best and to use empathy is to 'sugar coat'.

Since my own development (Kelley's) was focused on growing assertiveness and my default has been empathy, it is now the case that both my empathy and empathetic assertiveness can inform my questions for Jamie. My ability to think about situations from the other person's point of view and consider how they are feeling informs even how I feel for Jamie. Demonstrating empathy to Jamie for being seen as uncaring not only cares for Jamie but allows Jamie to experience my empathy.

My clear direct communication, feedback and questions around the negative impact from Jamie's assertive, un-empathetic communication with two colleagues and the team allow Jamie to consider aspects of relating that were never raised as an issue before.

One of Jamie's direct reports is Leena. To set the stage I want to tell you more about Leena. Leena is a dedicated employee at the company. Her specific role is as a network technician. She has been with the company for 11 years. Now she reports to Jamie.

Leena's Mom died when she was just 14 years old. She had been ill with cancer for 3 years. As the oldest child in her family Leena had to grow up fast and did a lot of caring for her two younger brothers.

At her job, Leena loves to work independently. She finds Jamie very detail-oriented. Jamie has been asking to be copied on many emails, demands to be included in significant meetings and wants to be notified when Leena is going to be out of the office. It feels like her new boss is a "control freak" and is micro-managing. She feels like Jamie is not appreciating all of her hard work and is not clueing in to how competent she is.

These requests from Jamie represent significant changes from how things were done and Leena really feels like she is not being valued or trusted. The impact on her well-being has been substantial. Meetings where she feels confronted about her professional behavior triggers lots of anxiety and she has been frequently taking personal/mental health days away from work.

Jamie would normally double down and ask for better performance, increased accountability and would normally report absences, etc. to HR as unapproved. However, HR has stepped in and asked Jamie to 'be more empathetic'.

Jamie is your client and you need to support growth in what the company wants to see for its culture but also growth that is ultimately healthy for Jamie. Where do you start?

Spotting Assertiveness and Empathy During Coaching

As a coach, what are some of the key words and behaviors that will help me know the level of assertiveness and level of empathy that my coachee is operating with?

Jamie used phrases like 'I'm just asking her to do her job'. 'She's been allowed to get away with non-performance'. 'Why should I have to be nice when she isn't meeting deadlines.' There are words and phrases that have a healthy or unhealthy impact and they are based on underlying assumptions. We've mentioned some already. Words or phrases like 'sugar-coating', accountability, not being someone's friend, insubordination. All of these words have a healthy version and an unhealthy version and much of what makes it unhealthy is determined by looking more closely at the two real people in the real situation.

Let's place you as Jamie's coach now. After having Jamie complete the EQ-i 2.0 assessment, you as the coach confirm that assertiveness is high but empathy is significantly lower. How would you as Jamie's coach support new thinking and new behaviors that use Jamie's assertiveness strength but incorporate more empathy?

Understandably Jamie is shocked by being confronted about abrasive behavior. This is the same behavior that has allowed a quick climb up the corporate ladder to this current management position. Initially, coaching may need to focus on increased self-awareness to allow Jamie to see how assertive requests and statements are being received by others and will also help him to further develop perspective-taking. Jamie also needs increased awareness about this new and very different organizational culture and how the same professional behaviors are viewed differently now.

Cognitive shifts in awareness make room for new perspectives and new behaviors.

Once Jamie has grown in understanding how assertiveness is being experienced in the new corporate culture it's time to start designing new behaviors, new conversations and new ways of listening to others. Incorporating more empathy allows Jamie to shift ways of thinking about others more quickly and allows for increased clarity about what new behaviors need to be part of this new role in order to get the same positive results received in prior management roles.

Jamie has been trying to adopt more of a coach approach with Leena. Asking her to talk more, listening and reflecting back what she is saying at an emotional level as well as on a factual level and paying attention to her body language cues.

Learning the language of healthy empathy is also something we have coached on. Healthy empathy means that I notice and care about how someone else is feeling then I make a conscious and informed choice about what I do next. Jamie is learning to use questions like "How can I support you during this stressful time so that we can meet our team deadline?" Jamie's authentic use of empathy will look different from mine. Jamie's strength in assertiveness will make for a powerful combination with new empathy skills really encouraging Leena to be her best and to reach her potential while having healthier boundaries.

Questions to Evoke Client Awareness

- Do your behavior choices equally respect your needs as well the needs of others?

- What would it look and sound like if you added a bit more assertiveness to your empathy?

- What are you feeling in this situation that you are uncomfortable saying out loud?

- When you show up with such deep empathy for others what are some of the patterns you notice?

- What is being high in assertiveness and lower in empathy costing you?

- How has assertiveness served you in the past, if at all?

- What is being so high in empathy and low in assertiveness costing you? How is it serving you, if at all?

Resources

As evidenced-based coaches we spend a fair amount of time reading the research available to us through the International Coaching Federation website and other coach-specific memberships such as the Institute of Coaching at McLean, a Harvard Medical School Affiliate. We are genuinely fascinated by the research on empathy and assertiveness being done in such diverse fields as law, business, psychology and social neuroscience to name only a few. Whether you take some time to better understand the role personality plays in our expressions of empathy and assertiveness or ways we can further develop these important social-emotional skills, we can say first hand that reading the associated research will be professional development time well-spent.

We also acknowledge that not everyone benefited as we did from wrestling with these two skills in particular over the course of their lives but you can take steps now to further develop your own empathy and assertiveness that will serve both you and your future clients. Perhaps you could start by identifying the areas of your life that could benefit from a bit more empathy or a bit more assertiveness and then, as we often suggest to our clients, experiment. Or you might want to register to take one of several emotional intelligence assessments available online or by a fellow coach or even enroll in a professional certification training. We've listed a few of our favorite resources below.

Books:

Burnout: The Secret To Unlocking The Stress Cycle. By Emily Nagoski, PhD., Emily Nagoski, DMA. 2019.

Emotional Intelligence: A 21 Day Step By Step Guide To Mastering Social Skills, Improve Your Relationships And Boost Your EQ. By David Clark. 2018.

Emotional Intelligence 2.0. By Travis Bradberry and Jean Greaves. 2009.

Mindset: The New Psychology Of Success. By Carol Dweck, PhD. 2006.

Mindwise: Why We Misunderstand What Others Think, Believe, Feel and Want. By Nicholas Epley. 2014.

Primal Leadership: Learning To Lead With Emotional Intelligence. By Richard Boyatzis, Daniel Goleman and Annie McKee. 2002.

The EQ Edge: Emotional Intelligence And Your Success. By Steven J. Stein, PhD. and Howard E. Book, M.D. 2011.

The EQ Leader: Instilling Passion, Creating Shared Goals and Building Meaningful Organizations Through Emotional Intelligence. By Steve J. Stein, PhD. 2017.

References:

Ames, Daniel R., Flynn,Francis J.. "What Breaks a Leader: The Curvilinear Relation Between Assertiveness and Leadership." Columbia.edu. Columbia University Journal of Personality and Social Psychology, 2007, Vol. 92, No. 2, 307–324.

Bar-On, Reuven. "The 15 Factors on the Reuven Bar-On Model." ReuvenBaron.org. 2013.

Craig, Heather. "17 Emotional Intelligence Tests and Assessments." PositivePsychology.com

2021.

Mnookin, Robert, Peppet, Scott, Tulumello, Andrew. "The tension between empathy and assertiveness." ResearchGate.net. 1996. Negotiation Journal.

Selva, Joaquín, Bc.S. "The Quick Guide to Assertiveness: Become Direct Firm and Positive." PositivePsychology.com. 2020.

Stern, Robin, Divecha, Dianna. "How to Avoid the Empathy Trap." GreaterGood.Berkley.edu.

7 July 2015. Greater Good Magazine, University of California at Berkeley.

Wyeth, Sims. "Two Opposing Skills No Leader Can Do Without." Inc.com. 2015.

Bios

Marilyn Orr *has been coaching since 2005 supporting executives, entrepreneurs, students and fellow coaches in Canada and the USA. Marilyn is a mentor coach and loves helping coaches as they pursue credentials and ongoing development.*

Speaking and training has been part of Marilyn's career for 25 years. Recent topics include emotional intelligence, leadership and coaching competencies - e.g. Emotional Intelligence and Conflict and Assertiveness + Empathy: Underutilized and Misunderstood. In 2019 Marilyn became a Training Partner with Multi-Health Systems, the developer of the EQ-i 2.0 assessment tool. She certifies professionals in correctly interpreting and using this emotional intelligence tool.

Marilyn believes that emotional intelligence growth is a big part of both resilience and leadership. Her extroverted personality comes out to play both one-on-one and with groups wanting to grow their skills. Clients report no judgment and laughing lots.

Recently she and her husband completed the creation of The Cedars Ranch, a sustainable event center focused on wellness. If you'd like to reach out to Marilyn for coaching around emotional intelligence, leadership or resilience feel free to visit her webpage:

https://www.capacitybc.com

Kelley Russell-DuVarney *is a Certified Positive Psychology Coach and Appreciative Inquiry practitioner committed to coaching individuals and teams interested in identifying new ways of thinking and behaving that allow them to more sustainably reach their goals. Kelley's background in Sociology allows her to notice both individual and institutional barriers alike that may prevent consistent progress. She is deeply committed to her own personal and professional development and believes her evidenced-based approach to coaching is a key differentiator.*

A native New Englander and a pragmatist at heart, her clients often share her preference for action and experimentation along with her use of metrics. She is the Past-President of the ICF-Greater Austin Chapter and currently serves on the Chapter's Advisory Council. When not at work you will find her out for a run, visiting with friends and neighbors or reading a book while sipping coffee at one of her favorite Austin, TX cafés. You can connect with Kelley on LinkedIn @kelleyrussellduvarney.

HOW TO GET THE ON-GOING FEEDBACK WE NEED AS COACHES

By Ted Middelberg, Ed.D., MBA

There is a very significant body of literature that well documents the importance of feedback for growing and learning. On an organizational level one of the more recognized thinkers was Peter Senge[1], who details *The Five Disciplines* that build a learning organization. On an individual level one of the seminal thinkers was Malcolm Knowles[2], who focused on the attributes of adult learners including the attributes of being self-motivated, experience-based and problem-focused. Research on both the organizational and the individual levels make it abundantly clear that feedback is a critical component for learning and growth.[3, 4, 5, 25]

We benefit from challenging ourselves whether as a new or a well-tenured coach by asking: **Are the actions and initiatives we are pursuing sufficient to support our on-going growth and learning needs?**

There is recognition, especially in Europe, that coaches and clients both derive benefits from the coach being in some form of relationship that provides ongoing feedback. In the United States, this recognition is increasing at a much slower pace. There has been a more significant growth in the number of executive coaches participating in coaching supervision programs[6, 7]. The on-going nature of the feedback is a key differentiator between pursuing CEU's or certifications versus supplementing those with a supportive feedback environment conducive for on-going feedback. I believe an on-going and supportive feedback environment is built on an open and trusting relationship. As Douglas Stone[8] put it, "All feedback is colored by the relationship between the giver and the receiver." My experience is that coaches optimize their effectiveness by being in these on-going professional relationships.

While in the role of coordinator for leadership development for Advanced Micro Devices' Austin campus, I was responsible for assessing developmental needs and delivering leadership training programs to address those needs. I thought I was pretty good at it. Then I asked some of the guys for feedback on a recent course I taught. They looked at me with a vague, distant expression and asked me to give them a hint as to what we had covered. Ouch! I then started designing in-action learning[9] concepts geared to ensuring they had the opportunity to practice what was being taught. That worked better than my simple class role-plays but this time the feedback was they did not know how to adapt what the class material covered to their real world situation. My next modification was adding in coaching sessions to support the iterations so essential for adult learning. This worked so well that it anchored my decision to become a leadership consultant and executive coach. The benefits of working in a rich feedback environment provided a pivotal difference in the effective transfer of knowledge from a classroom to their work context.

My research[10] in the late 1990's found that the pool of available and usable feedback was a critical variable in explaining the differing levels of team performance. As coaches, we partner with our clients in a thought provoking and creative process that inspires them to maximize their personal and professional potential[18] including serving as a resource to expand the pool of available and usable feedback for our clients within the safe space where vulnerability is expected. We co-create this feed-back environment replacing impoverished information with the best available information. The success of our work across all of our clients is highly dependent on the quality of the feedback environment co-created by the coach and the client. The creation of this space provides a highly valued, albeit invisible, resource to our clients.

Adult learning theory[2] suggests that our learning is enhanced by our levels of internal motivation. Motivations for coaches to expand our own feedback environment may vary widely including such generic categories as:

- Building skills and capabilities
- Driving better outcomes for the client
- Feeling wholeness and purpose (Parker Palmer *Let Your Life Speak*)
- Seeking greater presence (Doug Silsbee *Presence-Based Coaching*)
- Overcoming feeling stuck
- Differentiating through certification
- Enhancing personal and professional confidence
- Recognizing your own barriers to change
- Realizing our potential

Even with the best of motivations for creating their own feedback environment, the coach may not be as successful at getting the feedback he/she/they need to make progress. At the highest level, coaching is about helping the client change behaviors. From a systemic problem solving perspective, we work with our clients to clarify and define the problem area, locate that problem in their work context, co-create possible solutions, develop action plans to implement the solutions, evaluate the outcomes and design-in support for continued success. We can do the same work on ourselves. As adult learners and coaches, we want to clarify and define the areas where we want feedback.

How do we discover those areas where we would benefit from more insight? What are the early warning signals? In my own coaching work, there always seem to be a few rough spots where a bigger toolkit or more reflection would prove helpful. In our coaching role, we are constantly making judgments on how to interpret information, when to ask for examples, when to push back, when to offer feedback, when to share how we are feeling, when to reframe the issue, etc. There never seems to be a shortage of challenges that require increasing levels of growth and knowledge!

The definition of supervision used in this chapter follows that of the EMCC (European Mentoring and Coaching Council). "Supervision is the interaction that occurs when a mentor or coach brings their coaching or mentoring work experiences to a supervisor in order to be supported and to engage in reflective dialogue and collaborative learning for the development and benefit of the mentor or coach, their clients and their organizations."[6]

Peter Hawkins[11, 23, 24] developed a model for supervision called "The seven-eyed process model of supervision." This model derives its name by looking at the coaching engagement from seven different perspectives. The first four levels are most relevant for identifying early warning signals that could serve as the motivation for seeking on-going feedback. The last three levels are related to the feedback environment that has been co-created and how that can be used to stimulate further learning and growth. While I have identified a robust sample of these early warning signals based on my coaching experiences, you will have your own unique list based on your coaching experiences. I posit that identifying and articulating these in the context of current cases is one of the primary benefits of seeking ongoing feedback from a trusted colleague.

Level 1, The Client Situation. Here the focus is on how the coach understands the client and how they present as well as the relationship between the client and the organization.

> *Missed something*: In one case, as I reviewed my notes I discovered I didn't probe enough about the client's work context to fully understand and appreciate how serious the issue was that they were presenting. My motivation to seek feedback is often driven by curiosity about what I was missing that would give me a more congruent picture of the client's world.

> *Cultural Barriers:* Awareness of the culture and broader organizational context can be an important source of data for the coach. Knowing how the organization's values and assumptions impact the client can provide insight into what options are viable. Perhaps more importantly, increasing the client's awareness of these may help him/her/they realize it is not so personal or not just about them. These are sometimes hard to see – the phrase "fish don't see the water" comes to mind – which is exactly why we may benefit from working with a trusted third party or colleague.

Level 2, The Coach's Interventions. The focus is on strategies and interventions used by the coach.

> *Sure of myself:* The father of modern social psychology, Kurt Lewin[12], is often quoted as saying, "there is nothing more

practical than a good theory". Early in my career I would often feel quite certain I had it all figured out and forgot about the concepts of suspending judgment and framing the issues as a good theory or a working hypothesis. Now, I use the sense of righteous certainty as a clarion bell that something is amiss and so I seek out the inputs from a trusted colleague. My supervisor and I have explored questions such as, "Why I was so absolutely certain ...?" and "Where else have I got in trouble doing this ...?" and "What else is keeping me from forming alternative, viable hypotheses?" Tough questions!

Not sure of myself: At the other end of the spectrum there have been times where I felt uncertain as to what to do next. My interventions were not proving helpful. Many times this can be addressed by reviewing my notes and giving myself the gift of more reflection time. Other times I found a more efficient process required exploration with a colleague. Issues we discussed included conversations around gaps in our co-creation process where I was letting the client off the hook and taking on a role that was more comfortable for the client but that had the unintended consequence of creating an imbalance in how we were holding each other accountable.

Understanding their pickle: Clients often get themselves caught in dilemmas where their interests and intents do not align. Sometimes identifying these is straightforward and easy. At other times, we have both found ourselves stumbling around and missing the core dilemma. Whenever I felt like I was incorrectly framing the core dilemma, I also felt like the interventions we created were off the mark or a bit less potent and impactful. Just as we help our clients frame and reframe their issues, we as coaches can benefit from a neutral and trusted colleague helping us do this. In relationship with my supervisor, I was able to understand how I was not proactive enough in exploring the client's constraints to change. Since then I've so internalized that concept that in my current model of coaching I have included an explicit worksheet to help surface the constraints.

Level 3, Relationship between the Client and the Coach: The focus is on the system and relationship that the client and coach have co-created.

Too much in the system: A technique used in qualitative research is to hold a participant-observer stance where you are both a participant and have the ability to stand outside of the system looking in with an objective observer perspective. Losing that objectivity has had lots of implications on my work including my willingness to push or to support the client. The benefits of seeking external feedback can help restore the participant-observer balance we, as coaches, bring to the engagement. A trusted colleague can ask grounding questions with an invitation to look at the situation from above it and with less emotional engagement. I found this form of framing to be quite helpful in regaining my ability to see the whole system in context.

Relationship issues: There are clients that I enjoy spending time with, marked by an easy repartee and an open flow to the conversations. And there are other clients where that is not the case. Addressing these client-coach interface issues with a trusted colleague has proven to be very effective at addressing issues that I, the coach, bring into the engagement. The trusted colleague I sought out for a consultation pushed me to a deeper level of self-awareness with questions such as, "What exactly is causing this reaction in you?" and "What is the cost of not sharing that with your client?" While I struggled to answer these questions, that was exactly what I needed to do.

Level 4, The Coach. The focus is on the coach and what is being restimulated or triggered by the engagement.

Keeps me up: When I find the same unresolved issue intruding into my consciousness, without a clear plan for resolution, it is a strong signal that I do not have the internal resources to fully understand or explore the issue. There are typically so many moving parts that underlie these issues that I most often want to bounce those against a trusted colleague before bringing my concerns and insights into the client space. That can feel like having a friend help me untangle a Gordian knot.

My emotions: As coaches, we are not expected to be unemotional others to be used as the client's self-object. In fact, quite the opposite is true if we are to be in an authentic relationship with our clients. Clients will stir things up in me that, if left unattended, could preclude me from being fully present with them. Yvonne Agazarian[13], author of *Systems Centered Training* and founder of the Systems Centered Training Institute, used to always ask us what was going on in our bodies based on the belief that our bodies knew before our brains did. I found this to be sage advice and an indicator that there is an area that would benefit from further work. I find that now years after her training, I still miss some of my physiological signs, e.g. foot tapping, teeth grinding, tummy tightening. The good news is that the trusted colleagues I have used over the years for feedback are really good at spotting these as are my clients!

Here-and-now: The warning that I may need to consult with a trusted colleague and gain more personal awareness occurs when I find myself self-censoring rather than bringing my experiences into the room in a non-judgmental way. The client loses potentially valuable insights when I close off aspects of how I am feeling. An example would be when I found myself getting more and more agitated or impatient and did not bring that into the room. This links directly to the example above on attunement to how my body was reacting. One of my supervisors, with the softest of hands, asked me when I had given up on my client's ability to think himself out of his dilemma. Even with soft hands, there was a sting to the comment. However, the ensuing conversation led to a set of very constructive interventions that were anchored on the insights I had to offer.

Blind spots: This is the great unknown. Sometimes I'll find myself with a hint that something is amiss. It is as if the issue is right around the corner and I just cannot see it. A recent example was with a client who was trying to face his fears. Without even thinking about it, I dropped his signal that this emotion was important to him. It was only with the feedback from a trusted colleague that I gained an understanding of how important this may be for the client and insight into why I was avoiding his invitation to explore this feeling. My own experience and that of many coaches I know is that we find deep satisfaction when we can authentically attune and be present with our clients across a broadening range of issues, emotions and challenges.

Digging around: The simple act of reflecting on each coaching case and identifying two or three areas where I have some curiosity about how to improve is a solid discovery technique. It is as if those areas are always there just waiting to be discovered! Just the act of taking time to reflect on the case from an observer perspective has opened areas for further exploration.

With so many benefits to engaging with a trusted other to co-create a feedback environment, one should pause and explore the barriers to getting the feedback we need to grow and learn.

As Agazarian[13] pointed out, it is typically more efficient to address the barriers than to keep pushing on the driving forces.

What are the barriers to getting the on-going feedback we need to grow and learn?

Bad things can happen. Establishing the feedback environment, one marked by safety and trust, affords the opportunity to build relationships that can sustain the heavy lifting of sharing what is important. However, the research in the feedback field is replete with cautions on the risks of giving feedback[14, 15]. When I trained managers on the requisite skills for providing effective performance feedback, most participants had some visceral memory of how giving feedback went badly awry despite their good intentions. Most of us have not been taught how to give feedback in a way that effectively results in behavioral change[8].

Not wanted. Correspondingly, we usually do not learn how to ask for feedback in a way that provides the insights we need to make sustained change. The dysfunctional manager who does not want to hear anything that implies personal shortcomings is a familiar character. As one client phrased it, "We work awfully hard here to hide our weaknesses." However, both executives and coaches who understand the value of continuous improvement want and need feedback from others to increase self-awareness, an attribute that is strongly associated with effectiveness and an anchor point in our emotional intelligence [15, 16, 17].

Hard work. Doctor Atul Gawande[19] wrote a compelling article in the New Yorker on the impact coaching had on his surgical skills. Gawande was an accomplished surgeon whose complication rate was well below the national average; nonetheless, he was frustrated when he reached a plateau and was unable to figure out how to lower his rate of incidents. He convinced a retired surgeon and teacher to observe his operations and make suggestions on his techniques. His former teacher frequently proposed small changes that combined to make a big difference such as changing the way the surgical drape was placed to give the assistant a better reach and being conscious of how his elbow tended to rise at a certain point in the procedure. Dr. Gawande was surprised by the increased medical efficacy that was uncovered by the objective feedback from this trusted, knowledgeable colleague.

Relationship matters. The relationship between the person giving the feedback and the person receiving the feedback really matters. This relationship influences the ability to be receptive to the importance and usefulness of the feedback[19]. The perils of succumbing to someone who says, "I really want your honest feedback" are well known to most of us from personal and professional experiences. One client shared how he made a mistake with his boss. When I interviewed the boss, he described how my client had shown poor judgement in being offensively blunt. When I asked my client how that happened, he disclosed that this boss cajoled him into a false sense of openness. Colleagues and coaches willing to provide candid feedback make themselves vulnerable to creating ill will, challenge or even retribution.

Self exposure. On the other side, coaches and colleagues asking for feedback take the risk of disclosing goals that are especially salient to their success or of exposing areas they perceive to be weaknesses. They also risk being judged as uncertain or insecure. Ironically, while this risk may keep us from seeking feedback, the reality is that exposing oneself by seeking feedback that might be negative increases constituents' opinion of that person's overall effectiveness[5].

Requires risk taking. The two-way street of feedback is plagued by risks on both sides. It is precisely these risks that make developing safety and trust through relationships in a feedback environment so imperative. The business executive research is clear: better things happen when there are high-quality relationships with their managers. The opposite holds true as well: one of the most common reasons people provide for leaving an organization is a poor relationship with their manager. While the above research is from the business environment, I believe the underlying dynamics make it directly relatable to the coach's world. Most of us know coaches that just don't seem to be able to hold a long term engagement with their clients. While it could be a bad-fit or some skillset the coach lacks or characters within the client, it also could be that underneath those issues could be the client's perception that he/she/ they are not working in a safe and trusting relationship.

Too costly. There are lots of conversations among supervisors who are certified and seeking to expand their practice about what rates they should charge[20]. The recent Global Coaching Supervision Report[6] revealed that about two-thirds of the supervisors charged between $100 and $300 per hour. Many of the certified supervisors I know accept sliding scales. In my own coaching practice, I have embedded the cost of being supervised in the fees I charge the client. Starting a coaching practice and reaching economic viability is challenging. Providing a high level of service to our clients is also a challenge we all face. Finding the right balance across this apparent dilemma is important and up to the individual to decide. As my supervisor once asked me, "Have you considered the cost of not doing …?"

So far, this chapter has been about the motivations for entering into an on-going feedback relationship and some of the challenges or barriers you may have to address upon entering into such a relationship. Now, I'd like to address the question raised in the title of this chapter: **How to Get the On-Going Feedback We Need as Coaches.** I will offer four primary pathways to building the resourcing system we need to get on-going feedback we need to grow and learn.

1. Social contact with other coaches through local chap-

ter meetings, coaching events or voluntary coaching opportunities where you have the chance to interact with and get to know other coaches. A similar benefit can be found through organizations such as The Center for Creative Leadership where the coaches in any given city have periodic information sharing sessions. The idea is to go into "scan mode" in search of kindred spirits for both personal and professional growth. Having a favorable personal relationship is a great entry to building a professional relationship that supports the trust and safety we need for disclosing areas where we want feedback. These relationships can evolve into regular dyadic meetings to discuss the challenges both parties face in their coaching work.

2. A more structured, group approach was created by the local chapter under the leadership guidance of Kelley Russell-DuVarney,_with support from Sherry Lowry, Ted Middelberg, Marcia Rhode, Laura Di Tomasso and others. The benefits this MasterMind group approach offered were identified as ...

   a. You are listened-to in a safe and nonjudgmental environment.

   b. You have the support and encouragement of your fellow coaches.

   c. You dramatically increase your chances of resolving your coaching topic because a group of people will assist you in brainstorming solutions and action steps.

   d. You can bounce ideas off of the group before you implement an action saving yourself time, energy, money and aggravation.

   e. You receive helpful feedback from proactive, objective people who are invested in your success.

   f. You develop deeper relationships with other Austin coaches.

3. Enlist the for-hire mentoring services of someone who has the necessary training and skills that you are seeking. Mentor coaches are a great resource as they have been certified as competent at focusing their knowledge, skills and experience within the context of coaching competencies. I cannot overstate how valuable these qualified individuals have been in my own career. Several years ago, while presenting a tough case to my mentor, he caused me to gasp when he casually said, "So Ted, when did you give up on your client? Another "ouch" moment and time for deeper reflection! These individuals are well trained to ask the tough and most important questions.

4. The last resource is engaging in a coaching supervision training program or hiring a coach who has completed a coaching supervision program. The role of the supervisor is different from that of the mentor. Whereas the domain of knowledge for the mentor is anchored by the coaching competencies, the knowledge domain of the supervisor is more holistic and systemic [18, 22, 23, 24, 26]. Earlier in this page, I covered the first four levels of Hawkin's Seven-Eyed Model. The upper three levels (5, 6 and 7) add additional insights that can further benefit the coach's effectiveness.

Level 5, The Relationship. The focus is what is happening in the room between the   supervisor and the coach they are working with.

> *Parallel processes:* A term parallel process is used to describe the pattern of relations in one area enacted in another area without our conscious awareness. That is, something the client does or says triggers an old emotional memory in me that could get in the way of being fully present with the client. An example shared by Peter Hawkins[11] is the supervisor saying, "I am feeling judged as though I have to come up with the right answer right now.   I wonder if that is how you feel with your coachee?"

> *Level 6, The Supervisor.* At this level the supervisor benefits by paying attention to how they are feeling and reacting in the here-and-now with the coach they are supervising. And then they bring that information into the conversation. A descriptive example is the supervisor feeling impatient and asking the coach if that could be connected in any way. Level 6 invites the supervisor to serve as sounding board for what else is going on but is not being directly addressed in their conversations.

> *Level 7, Wider Context.* This level is intended to raise awareness of all the other things going on that can impact our coaching work. These could include organizational, social, cultural or ethic contexts. Some of the cultural/ organizational areas of concern are how the firm handles conflict and disagreement and how the wider political, economic and social events (think Covid-19!) are influencing the coach's working relationship.

While there are other approaches to the four pathways or feedback possibilities listed above for levels 1-4 suggesting how a coach can create an environment to get the systemic feedback they need to grow and learn, it strikes me as important to create your own feedback environment. The importance of the coach building relationships with someone they would turn to for creating the feedback environment is strengthened by new research in neurophysiology and attribution theory. Recent research by Stephen Porges[21] in the field of neurophysiology applied to social engagements explains how a perceived lack of safety can push us past/flight responses all the way to immobilization. The neurophysiology research has determined that, as part of our social engagement system, we assess for safety before we selectively turn off our defenses.

This aligns with my own research, experience coaching, supervising other coaches, and being supervised by other coaches. When we create a feedback environment marked by high levels of safety and trust we are more likely to replace defensive routines with openness, curiosity and a willingness to make ourselves vulnerable to taking risks. Relationships matter because those expand the basis for safety and trust which in turn enables others to take the risks of being vulnerable and sharing information that might be hard to hear.

Bibliography

1. Peter Senge, P. (2006) Second Edition. *The Fifth Discipline: The Art & Practice of the Learning Organization*

1. Knowles, M. S., Holton III, E. F., Swanson, R. A. (8th Edition , 2015) *The Adult Learner: The definitive classic in adult education and human resource development.*

3. Ilgen, D.R., Fisher, C.D., & Taylor, M.S. (1979). "Consequences of individual feedback on behavior in or-

ganizations." *Journal of Applied Psychology*, 64(4), 349-371.

4. Morrison, E.W., & Bies, R.J. (1991). "Impression management in the feedback-seeking process: a literature review and research agenda". *Academy of Management Review*, 16 (3), 522-541.

5. Ashford, S.J., & Tsui, A.S. (1991). "Self-regulation for managerial effectiveness: The role of active feedback seeking". *Academy of Management Journal*, 34(2), 251-280

6. McAnally, K., Abrams, L., Asmus, M. J., Hildebrandt, T. (2020) *GLOBAL COACHING SUPERVISION: A Study of the Perceptions and Practices Around the World,* 2020, Retrieved on the web at https://coachingsupervisionresearch.org/wp-content/uploads/2020/02/Global_Coaching_Supervision_Report_FINAL.pdf

7. Personal communications with Damian Goldvarg, Goldvarg Consulting Group.

   https://goldvargconsulting.com/executive-coaching/coaching-supervision-certification/

8. Stone, D. & Heen, S. (2014) *Thanks for the Feedback: The science and art of receiving feedback well.* Penguin Group, NY NY

9. Marquardt, M.J. (1999). *Action Learning in Action:*

Transforming Problems and People for World-Class Organizational Learning. Palo Alto, CA: Davis-Black Publishing.

10. Middelberg, T.M. (1999). *The relationship between leader behaviors and job satisfaction and collective efficacy.* Unpublished Dissertation. The University of Texas at Austin.

11. Hawkins, P. & Smith, N. (2013). Second Edition. *Coaching, Mentoring and Organizational Consultancy: Supervision, Skills and Development.* McGraw Hill Open University Press

12. Lewin, K. (1999). *The Complete Social Scientist: A Kurt Lewin Reader, 1st ed.* Gold, M. (Ed.). Washington, DC: American Psychological Association.

13. Agazarian, Y.M. (2004). *Systems-Centered Therapy for Groups.* London, England: Karnac Books.

14. Morrison, E.W., & Bies, R.J. (1991). "Impression management in the feedback-seeking process: a literature review and research agenda." *Academy of Management Review,* 16 (3), 522-541.

15. Folkman, J.R., (2006). *The Power of Feedback.* John Wiley & Sons. NY NY

16. Goleman, D., & Boyatzis, R. (2008). "Social intelligence and the biology of leadership." *Harvard Business*

Review, September, 2008, 74-81.

17. Siegel, D. J. (2010). *Mindsight: The New Science of Personal Transformation.* New York, NY: Random House.

18. Cochrane, H. & Newton, T. (2018) *Supervision and Coaching: Growth and Learning in Professional Practice.* Routledge, NY, NY.

19. (2020) Personal communications between Ted Middelberg and other certified coaching supervisors.

20. Porges, S.W. (2011). *The Polyvagal Theory: Neurophysiological Foundations of Emotions, Attachment, Communication, and Self-regulation.* New York, NY: W.W. Norton.

21. Gawande, Atul. (October 3, 2011). "Personal Best." *The New Yorker.* Retrieved from http://www.newyorker.com/reporting/2011/10/03/111003fa_fact_gawande?currentPage=all

22. Hawkins, P. & Shohet, R. (2012, Fourth Edition) *Supervision in the Helping Professions.* McGraw Hill Open University Press. NY, NY.

23. Bachkirova, T., Jackson, P., and Clutterbuck, D. (2011) *Coaching & Mentoring Supervision: Theory and Practice.* McGraw-Hill Open University Press. NY, NY.

24. Hawkins, P & Turner, E. (2020). *Systemic Coaching: Delivering value beyond the individual.* Routledge Press. NY, NY.

25. Buckingham, M & Goodall, A. (March-April 2019) "Why Feedback Fails" *Harvard Business Review.* Pp. 92-101.

26. Hay, J. (2007). Reflective Practice and Supervision for Coaches. McGraw Hill, Open University Press

Bio

Ted Middelberg, Ed.D., MBA

President, Transformational Executive Coaching, LLC

Middelberg is a certified executive coach and certified coaching supervisor with over 20 years of executive coaching experience. The genesis for his firm, Transformational Executive Coaching, was his search for what executive coaches do that really matters.

His approach to coaching is built on goal-focused processes that drive and sustain the dramatic changes that leaders want from a coaching engagement. His desire is to help executives build their toolkit in ways that support both personal and organizational success.

He has found that the process works best when there is a high degree of trust and rapport between the two parties, coachee and coach. He builds the holding environment that enables the executive to take perspective as well as explore blind-spots and behaviors that may no longer serve his/her goals. Coaching and supervising coaches is also about accepting the discomfort of change and helping the client achieve important goals. Similarly, it is about having fun learning and growing together.

You can contact Ted at 512-653-4757 or at ted@teccoaches.com. Further information is available at www.teccoaches.com.

THE DOING OF COACHING

BREAKING THROUGH THE AWARENESS BARRIERS

By Kandice Klumb, MA, ACC

INTRODUCTION

Why is self-awareness important and what makes gaining it so challenging?

You may be familiar with the Ancient Greek principle, "Know Thyself." Socrates taught that "self-knowledge is the key to wisdom." From Socrates and Sun Tzu to Aquinas and Freud, self-awareness has remained an important theme for philosophers throughout history.

As a coach and leadership development professional, I believe that self-awareness is the foundation to successful clients, successful leaders, successful teams and more fulfilled humans. After all, if you don't know where you are and where you would like to go, how are you going to get there?

For our purposes, we will define *self-awareness* as: the conscious understanding of who you are, who you want to be, how you fit into the world and how others see you. Before individuals can feel ownership of their life, they need to be aware of what their values, aspirations and strengths are. Before leaders can spark action in others, they need to gain insight to what drives them. Greater self-awareness can lead to greater understanding and acceptance of others[1], more effective collaboration and deeper connection which can prove invaluable in our interdependent world.

Gaining self-awareness is not always easy. In fact, there are several barriers that can make the process of introspection more challenging or prevent the pursuit of greater self-awareness altogether.

As coaches, we play the crucial role of partnering with our clients to help spark their awareness of self, of their environment and ultimately possibilities that weren't previously visible. To be better prepared to help our clients overcome the potential pitfalls, let's examine them more closely and look at techniques to help overcome them.

BARRIERS TO SELF-AWARENESS

While not an exhaustive list, we will look at three common areas that can make the journey of awareness so challenging: how self-evaluation can lead to avoidance; how limiting beliefs and biases can get in the way; and how introspection can manifest as reflection or rumination.

Avoiding self-awareness due to discrepancy between current & ideal self

When we start to focus on ourselves it is very common to compare what we see to our ideal representation of it.[2] This can include physical representations like when summer begins and we try our bathing suit on for the first time. This can also include our ideal skills or personality characteristics. We might have a mentor we want to emulate or we may have the desire to be more outgoing. In any case, identifying the gap between our current state and desired state is the first step toward reducing the discrepancy. When the discrepancy is small, we might eliminate it by modifying ourselves or modifying our standards. If the discrepancy is too large, however, it can be unpleasant enough to lead to avoiding further introspection altogether or even escape.

As a new mother at 36, I struggled. I wanted to be 'the superhero' who had boundless energy, prepared the most nutritious meals, always had a clean house, had never ending patience and ran a full-time coaching business. In reality I was tired, often turning to breakfast for dinner and resisted the fact that I needed help with childcare if I was going to commit time to my career. There were evenings where wine won over self-work. While this is a toned down example of escape, it is a common example of how difficult it can be to address perceived shortcomings when they feel insurmountable thus leading us to avoid self-focus.

Avoidance can also occur when our actions don't align with our values. A client was working in an environment where 'you had to put your boxing gloves on daily' and fight to get your work done. A new leadership team had formed who were not well-aligned and they started gossiping about one another. My client found herself participating in this behavior which was contradictory to her values of collaboration, enthusiasm and integrity. It wasn't until she realized this that she understood why she had felt so drained and was working so hard to ignore the problems.

Finally, this avoidance of cognitive dissonance can also show up with self-other discrepancies. In a group coaching session we looked at a personality based assessment. One of the senior leaders had a strong emotional response to the results of the assessment. Some of the traits that were pointed out were so far from her desired state that even considering their possibility was shocking. She elected not to use the personality model within her team.

In a similar team coaching engagement, there was an individual who also had a strong reaction to seeing results that he didn't find favorable or true. However, his team rated them as 90-100% accurate which was not easy for him to hear and especially accept. He ended up leaving the company. This hurdle can be particularly relevant when coaching clients through 360-type assessments with many raters who have different relationships to the individual.

As coaches, while we are used to helping our clients by examining the gaps, asking questions about both current and ideal states, helping them decide how important it is to close any gaps, identifying potential changes that the client believes are possible and helping create action plans. Most importantly, we can understand how difficult introspection can be and provide a safe space for our clients to get curious and fully explore.

Below are a few sample questions that might be helpful in starting to uncover and overcome the avoidance that large discrepancies between the real and ideal self can bring.

- What are your strengths that you are most excited about?
- What are the things you value most?
- What qualities would describe your idea of ideal?
- On a scale of 1 to 10 (1 being 'not at all like me', 10 'exactly like me') how would you rate yourself in each of those areas?
- Which are most important to you?
- How would life be different if this area changed?
- How might you utilize your strengths to help you take action toward this goal?
- How does this goal align with your values?
- How would others describe you?
- What about that feedback is incorrect?

- Imagine for a moment that that opinion is correct, what is different?

- What is the worst case scenario?

- What is the best case?

- How do you want to move forward?

Limiting Beliefs

Another barrier can show up as firmly held beliefs that are either undoubtedly false or can't be proven and are holding our clients back.[3] Early 1900s actor Will Rogers had it right when he said, "It isn't what we don't know that gives us trouble, it's what we know that ain't so."

Limiting beliefs are profoundly common and are so in-grained in us that they are hard to spot on our own. They also can be difficult to change as we have spent our lifetime developing and reinforcing our views and beliefs. Questioning our beliefs can open completely new possibilities, opportunities and ways of thinking.

Our biases are contributors to these beliefs as they tend to reinforce them and make them more difficult to alter. Availability bias, whereby we judge frequency by the ease that instances come to mind and confirmation bias, whereby we seek data that is compatible or confirms our current beliefs, are just a couple examples.[4] Both biases can have implications on how we self-report certain instances of our own behavior. They can impact the information we get from personality reports. For example, if we start to seek behaviors that confirm what we have been told that we are, then we can be blinded by confirmation bias. Ultimately, biases impact the way we interpret the world around us, predict outcomes and they can keep us from our potential.

My husband and I met in graduate school where one of his favorite questions during class debates was "Why do you think

that?" The topics were often emotionally charged so feeling chal-
lenged was usually infuriating. After all, 'I just knew!' Going
home and reflecting on that question, however, offered me a gift.
I had the opportunity to become more conscious of where my
beliefs came from and what assumptions and interpretations I
was making to inform them.

A client wanted to work on gaining confidence in interviews
as she was ready to get a new job. Early in our engagement we
discovered that she had adopted a belief when she was young
that you are not supposed to talk about your own strengths and
achievements because that is boastful and boastful is bad. We
found that her preferred belief was that she can be proud of
her accomplishments and share them openly to allow the hiring
manager to assess fit. We looked at how she could share information about herself that is valuable to the hiring manager, including her strengths, while keeping boastfulness at bay.

Another client had been asked to submit a resume for a
newly created position. The position would now be oversee-
ing her department. The limiting belief that she adopted when
hearing the request was, 'You are actually not that qualified to
do this; otherwise, we would have simply promoted you to this
role.' This belief discouraged her from applying.

Imagine a client saying any of the following and how these
beliefs could make it difficult for them to get to where they want
to go.

"There is no other company with this flexibility."

"I'm not valued enough to get a raise."

"If I set boundaries with my manager then I could get fired."

"I am unhappy here but I just have to deal with it."

How do we help? The good news is that resisting limiting
beliefs, self-deception and bias is possible. We start by mak-

ing an effort to reconsider our impressions and intuitions. As coaches, we get to partner in a huge way and often help clients overcome this barrier. Reframing, exploring growth mindset, celebrating learning moments, having clients compare past predictions to actual outcomes and confronting assumptions are ways we help. This is also a good time to introduce or remind how thoughts, feelings, and actions are related.

A few sample questions that might also help in unveiling biases and limiting beliefs include:

- How has that belief served you and limited you?
- What might be possible if you were to believe something different?
- What else might be true?
- What would you tell a friend who told you that?
- If this was your inner critic's message, how would your inner supporter respond?
- What is one thing you have learned this week?
- How can you celebrate the things you have accomplished?
- How confident are you that you can increase your knowledge and ability in that area?
- When has something turned out completely differently than you had predicted?

Introspection turning into Rumination

The tendency for an individual to focus on the self can take two forms: rumination or reflection. Rumination is the tendency to focus on negative self-perceptions and emotions while reflection is the tendency to be objective.[5]

There are a few things that can lead to rumination: we focus on negative self-perceptions the majority of the time; we are too heavily focused on the past; or we are too concentrated on getting answers to unconscious motivations or reasons for feelings and behaviors.

Organizational Psychologist, Tasha Eurich, introduced the idea of *"knowledge blindness,"* *"emotional blindness"* and *"behavioral blindness."* In other words, we can't always assess what we know, how we feel or how we behave. She found that the question *"why"* is often associated with rumination.[6] When we ask *why* we feel the way we do we tend to generate reasons that follow our current beliefs. We typically do not recognize that those reasons are incomplete or inaccurate.[7] Instead of asking *why*, ask *what*: 'what can I do differently, what do I want, what are the situations that make me feel terrible and what do they have in common?'

A client who was trying to get a promotion had clearly defined goals with her boss but started to obsess over every 'mistake' that she made in meetings and over things that she didn't say. The presentation where she answered incorrectly kept playing over and over again in her head. After realizing that the thoughts were making her more anxious, she decided to work on getting more sleep, making time each week where she learned something new about her field and putting a morning routine of breathing into place. She went from ruminating to focusing on things that energized her that were within her control.

We can educate clients about the dangers of rumination which can help them start to recognize when they are ruminating and make conscious decisions about how to move forward. It is worth noting that rumination is a core process of depression and sometimes clients may need to be referred to therapy.[8]

There is preliminary support that practicing mindfulness can decrease the likelihood that a negative mood will spiral.[9] Using a mix of generic and personality based training may also be helpful here.[10]

When we are able to admit to our failings and put our successes in perspective, we can more easily reflect. The following questions may also help.

- What are you learning about yourself?
- What lessons can you take from the experience?
- How have you overcome similar challenges and experiences?
- How do you want to move through this?
- What do the situations that make you feel worse have in common?
- What physically happens in your body when you have that thought?
- What brings you joy?

CONCLUSION

One of my favorite quotes comes from Chinwe Esimai of Citigroup. She said, "The one constant factor in all your endeavors is you; understanding yourself is therefore paramount."

We are all working to some degree on creating a coherent self-narrative that suits us. Self-awareness has positive implications but it isn't always easy. Having increased confidence, increased creativity and an increased sense of identity and purpose are a few of the benefits that come from gaining an understanding and acceptance of yourself.

That said, rumination, avoidance and limiting beliefs are just a few of the things that can get in the way. The good news is that by simply knowing the potential barriers we are one step closer to getting past them. A few of the keys to successfully building self-awareness are having the right mindset, getting precise and meaningful feedback often[11] and being willing to test your own assumptions.

To become self-aware, one needs to gain insight into the following questions: Who am I? Who do I want to be? How do I fit into the world? How do others see me?

As coaches, we can help clients with structured introspection, activities to help see oneself through other's eyes, questions promoting self-observation/reflection and action planning that allows for application of what has been learned. It is important not to forget that we also have to continue to work, recognize and grow in these areas.

Here are a few questions for a quick start to building self-awareness together with your clients:

- What are your top five values?

- If there were no obstacles to overcome, what do you most want?

- What is one thing that you have learned about yourself this week?

- What do you do for fun?

- When do you find yourself in *flow*?

- How would others describe you?

- What are some common things you notice about how you behave in those situations?

- On a scale of 1 to 10 (1 being 'not at all', 10 being 'extremely') how clear are your goals to you?

I will leave you with this quote from Ralph Waldo Emerson, "Our chief want in life is somebody who shall make us do what we can." Coaches, you are the partners, the inspirers, the space holders. Wishing you well on your journeys.

[1] Sutton, Anna, Williams, Helen M. and Allinson, Christopher W. "A longitudinal, mixed method evaluation of self-awareness training in the workplace." *European Journal of Training and De-*

velopment 39.7 (2015): pg. 625

[2] Morin, Alain. "Self-Awareness Part 1: Definition, Measures, Effects, Functions, and Antecedents." *Social and Personality Psychology Compass* 5.10 (2011): 807-823

[3] Pennebaker, James (2011). *The Secret Life of Pronouns: What Our Words Say About Us.* Chapter 6.

[4] Kahneman, Daniel. *Thinking, fast and slow.* Farrar, Straus and Giroux, 2011.

[5] Sutton, Anna, Williams, Helen M. and Allinson, Christopher W. "A longitudinal, mixed method evaluation of self-awareness training in the workplace." *European Journal of Training and Development* 39.7 (2015): 610-627

[6] Eurich, Tasha. *Insight : the surprising truth about how others see us, how we see ourselves, and why the answers matter more than we think.* Currency. 2017. pg. 100

[7] Wilson, Timothy D and Elizabeth W Dunn. "SELF-KNOWLEDGE: Its Limits, Value, and Potential for Improvement." *Annu. Rev. Psychol* 55 (2004): 493-518.

[8] Sutton, Anna, Williams, Helen M. and Allinson, Christopher W. "A longitudinal, mixed method evaluation of self-awareness training in the workplace." *European Journal of Training and Development* 39.7 (2015): 610-627.

[9] Deyo, Mary, Wilson, Kimberly, Ong, Jason and Koopman, Cheryl. "Mindfulness and Rumination: Does Mindfulness Training Lead to Reductions in the Ruminative Thinking Associated With Depression?" *Explore* 5.5 (2009). pg. 270

[10] Sutton, Anna, Williams, Helen M. and Allinson, Christopher W. "A longitudinal, mixed method evaluation of self-awareness training in the workplace." *European Journal of Training and Development* 39.7 (2015): 610-627.

[11] Krajc, M, et al. "Are the unskilled really that unaware? An al-

ternative explanation." *Journal of Economic Psychology* 29 (2008): 724-738.

Bio

Kandice is a Certified Professional Coach who specializes in leadership development and wellbeing. She has spent the past 10 years focusing on people development. Her experience includes spending four years learning about cross-cultural communication, adult learning methodology, and navigating change in Da Nang, Vietnam and Buenos Aires, Argentina. She has researched the benefits, barriers, and methods of increasing self-awareness in relation to leadership effectiveness and overall satisfaction and developed and implemented leadership curriculum for leaders in 40+ countries.

Kandice works through her coaching, consulting, and training to help increase awareness & confidence, grow skill sets, and shift mindsets to create more satisfied and energetic people. She believes that more engaged people, teams, and organizations lead to happier, healthier, and more connected communities where we all want to live. Visit https://klumbllc.com to learn more.

YOUR "NEED TO KNOW" ABOUT EMOTIONAL INTELLIGENCE

By Marilynn Orr, PCC

Emotional Intelligence Summarized

You would have to live a very disconnected life to not be hearing about emotional intelligence these days. The fact that this topic comes up so much also means that the abundance of information, models, experts, books and mentions of it can lead to confusion and overwhelm about where to start.

In this chapter I'd like to pull together the big picture for you, show you how you are already doing emotional intelligence work with your clients and leave you with some growth steps and ideas for yourself and for your clients.

Let's start with what emotional intelligence is.

EQ or emotional intelligence quotient is the equivalent to IQ but on the emotional and social side of functioning. In the same way that an IQ measure is looking at a number of sub-skills, so is EQ. IQ includes math skills, spatial perception, language abilities, problem solving and memory. What does EQ look at?

The skills that make up emotional intelligence account for big parts of whether we are happy or not, for the quality of our relationships, for overall 'well-being'. EQ looks at a combination of skills that help us with emotional information, social dynamics and coping with problems and stress when emotion is involved. It is both about perceiving and choosing appropriate behaviors.

There are a variety of models on EQ that range in complexity from 4 categories to 15 but all focus on the same basic concepts. This article will not focus on one specific model although many examples will come from my more informed knowledge of the Multi-Health Systems, Inc. (MHS) EQ-i 2.0 model. My hopes for you as you read this chapter is that the main concepts make more sense to you and that you finish with more practical applications. I have found that going deep on one model (the MHS model which is based on the Bar-On model) really equips me with more tools, a deeper understanding and a better ability to support my own and my clients' growth.

The main models currently in EQ are Goleman's EI performance model, Bar-On's EI competencies model, and Mayer, Salovey, and Caruso's EI ability model. More recently Mark Brackett at the Yale Center for Emotional Intelligence has created a model being taught primarily to students called RULER which focuses on understanding emotions better and learning how to use them wisely.

Emotional Intelligence Buckets

Time to unpack this. Whatever categories a model uses there are overlaps between categories and interplay between them. The "buckets" help us hold the bigger concepts but the interplay between skills is quite prevalent and very meaningful. Each model packages differently but covers some core concepts:

- Perceiving emotions in myself and in others
  - The models use words like emotional self-awareness, recognizing emotion, self-awareness or social awareness strategies and empathy
- Understanding and responding to emotions
  - Here we can include the concepts of assertiveness and empathy (both include both awareness/perception and response), awareness of both cause and consequences around emotions in self and others, impulse control, independence, appropriate emotional expression and self-regard
- Regulation of emotional response
  - Included are concepts like emotional expression, self-management strategies, regulation of emotions, stress management, and optimism
- Relationship impacts
  - Concepts include social responsibilities, empathy, assertiveness, interpersonal mutual satisfaction measures and flexibility
- Decision Making

- Emotional self-awareness, flexibility, reality testing, impulse control, empathy and assertiveness all impact decision making

- Stress Management
  - Component concepts include optimism, flexibility, assertiveness, self-regard and impulse control.

As you can tell, the interplay and overlap is very prevalent between concepts, categories and skills. The beauty of some of these models happens when we start to actually consider two or more concepts side by side. Other factors can exaggerate or moderate the dynamics. There are limitless possibilities here but let's walk through a few to give you the idea and get your creative juices going on this concept.

Separately in this book Kelley Russell DuVarney and I dedicate a whole chapter to the interplay and power of Empathy and Assertiveness. Many of these specific skills juxtaposed to another create interesting windows for increasing awareness and motivation for personal and professional development.

Three Coaching Scenarios

Let's look at three examples. Likely this will start bringing to mind the coaching work you do with clients.

Scenario #1 - Imagine an individual that is:

- really high in emotional expression
- quite low in impulse control

What will we likely see?

- speaking before thinking
- sharing raw emotional content before processing
- emotional decision-making
- possibly angry outbursts
- potentially a lot of TMI sharing
- impulse shopping
- poor relationship boundaries

What might coaching focus on?

- More appropriate tools for emotional expression such as journaling or specific relationships and times designated for deep sharing

- Building in pauses before action, be that the old 'count to 10' or deep breaths or literally committing to separating out impulses from actions, e.g. 24 hours of wanting to buy something before actually choosing to buy it.

- Self-validation of emotions instead of expressing to others in order to grow internal validation skills. This may include learning some self-soothing techniques.

- Discussions around healthy boundaries, how to know how much to share when and where, establishing and honoring trust in a relationship and permission based sharing and advice-giving.

- Models for decision-making that include objective data as well as emotional information.

- Conversations around impact on both the coachee and on

their relationships from this pattern - at home, at work, with friends, etc.

- Conflict skills including better listening skills.

Tools for coaching this client:

Tool #1 - The L.A.E.R. model technique for conflict and communications can be very helpful. It helps with slowing down communication, becoming a better listener and allowing space for emotions to come out more constructively.

1. **Listen.** Give the other person your undivided attention. This is listening without interrupting, advising, fixing or getting defensive.

2. **Acknowledge.** Paraphrasing, reflecting and stating back to the speaker what you heard both in factual content and emotional content.

3. **Explore.** Use open ended questions, statements such as 'tell me more' and body language to encourage the speaker to continue. After you ask for more or clarifying information, actively listen again.

4. **Respond.** After repeating steps 1-3 as many times as needed for the other person to feel heard and for emotions to calm down it may be appropriate to offer a response.

Tool #2 - Co-creating some journaling questions to help the client self-validate emotions is a useful exercise. Just having someone journal is not always as effective as really helping them generate the questions that will help them the most. Figuring out either a frequency for journaling or how to recognize when journaling would be beneficial supports clients with low impulse control and/or high emotional expression.

Scenario #2 - Imagine an individual that is:

- Low in self-regard
- High in flexibility

What will we likely see?

- willingness to change plans for others
- likely some significant negative self-talk
- decision-making difficult with lots of second guessing
- may seek excessive external validation
- flexibility may be used to reduce stress - may live with anxiety
- flip-flopping on plans
- likely many relationships with controlling or abusive individuals
- happiness may be limited due to low self-regard

What might coaching focus on?

- Growing self-compassion
- Increasing emotional self-awareness to increase clarity on coachee's opinion
- Reflecting on core values and beliefs
- Supporting appropriate independence
- If assertiveness is low, growing it will help this person
- Setting healthy boundaries

Tools for coaching this client:

Tool #1 - Self-reflection exercises to help the client increase awareness of their own opinions, values, beliefs, desires and preferences. On-line there are easily accessible values exercises. core belief activities, etc. Helping this client get a strong sense of self will help give them something more concrete to weigh their decisions against.

Tool #2 - Self-compassion goes a long way. Dr. Kristin Neff (out of Austin, TX) has a number of helpful resources including a self-compassion assessment tool, videos, books and a workbook all on understanding and growing self-compassion. These are easy to find on-line.

Scenario #3 - Imagine an individual that is:

- High in emotional self-awareness
- Low in emotional expression

What will we likely see?

- An individual possibly reluctant to share
- Possibly flattened affect, muted tone, body language
- Relationships suffering due to lack of mutual intimate sharing

What might coaching focus on?

- Growing awareness of how much self-protection is happening keeping feelings private

- Understanding what makes sharing emotion feel safer and practicing in coaching

- This gap may be indicative of having been hurt, explore to move forward more safely

- Boundaries and how to set them

- Learning the indicators for how much is safe to share, who is safe to share with, etc.

Tools for coaching this client:

Tool #1 - Work with the coachee's high level of emotional self-awareness and have them journal or express in some other way the variety and depth of feelings they have about a specific situation. If they are willing, have them share this in coaching, a safe space. This alone is a big win. You can explore with them what the different elements are about the coaching relationship that allow them to feel safer. This can help them learn to look for the cues in other spaces.

Tool #2 - Ask the coachee to make a list of the different messages, overt and covert, they have received that reinforce that they should not or it is not safe to share their feelings. Are there cultural contributions? Gender? Age? Then walk with them through what the costs to them and to the people and organizations around them have been. Then, of course, discuss what the benefits could be of being 'seen, heard and understood' more.

Growth Steps for Coaches

When we help our clients strategize about being taken more seriously, set better boundaries at work or in their personal lives, work on self-sabotaging patterns or just work on knowing how they feel about something we are doing emotional intelligence coaching work. How can you be better equipped for this work?

First of all, work on you!

The best emotional intelligence growth we can get is not from a book! It is by setting stretch goals, experimenting with new behaviors, getting honest feedback and trying out new ways of showing up in the world. This is the work that we ask of our clients. This is the work that we need to do too.

Early on in my life all of these tools would have shown very low assertiveness levels for me. Although personality, birth order, culture, gender and family dynamics etc. may all play a part in why you show up as you do now, the truth is we can change our emotional intelligence and bring greater balance. By the time I first studied the MHS EQ-i 2.0 tool my assertiveness was my highest strength.

What are your strengths in emotional intelligence?

Which two or three areas would you most like to grow?

Pick a model and get familiar with it!

Models help us go deeper with concepts. They give us a framework for growth. Each model has resources to go with it to help you and to help your clients grow. EQ work is all about growing so there are many practical tools that go with most models.

One way to get more familiar is to take the assessment that likely goes with the model. Not all models offer this but most do. Get a sense of your own strengths, weaknesses, preferences and gaps.

I love lining up the emotional intelligence sub-skills with the ICF core competencies. This is a great exercise to help you understand where emotional intelligence growth can really impact your coaching competencies in general.

If you find that you love working with your clients in this area, consider getting certified in using one of these tools. This will absolutely take you deeper in your understanding but also in how you can support your clients' growth. Alternatively many certified coaches can complete the assessment for your client and debrief you and your client together on their results.

Who can you get more information about models from?

What books can you read to help you learn specific frameworks or about emotional intelligence in general?

Start to notice EQ skills (or lack thereof) with your clients.

Start to make observations that help you be more thorough and intentional in your coaching. For example, if I notice low impulse-control I'm going to get curious about how emotionally self-aware my client is. I will also want to see how assertive they are. Are they pushing their impulsive ideas on the people around them?

Start to compile your own list of questions, tools, books and activities that can help you help your coachees. Many tools from one model can easily apply in another model.

Whether it is this platform of emotional intelligence or coaching in general I am always consciously looking for the strengths that my client brings so that I can leverage that strength to support the areas where they want to grow. You can do the same thing.

For example, many of my coaches are extremely skilled at using logical and analytical thinking but struggle with empathy. Although we can look at the research on why empathy matters, there will be much better buy-in by clients if we can approach the topic through the lens they use to view the world already. Help them see logically and analytically what makes empathy so important. With questions that allow for increased awareness and 'aha' moments the coachee begins to design how to grow empathy since it has become logical to them to do so. Their own strengths and values provide a much more robust way forward than anything we could say.

Which of the emotional intelligence strengths in your coachee will help them grow the weaker areas?

Growth Steps for Coachees

Every person comes with different strengths and different areas that benefit from immediate focus. That said, I believe that there are a couple skills in particular that universally help to lay the foundation where we can build other EQ skills.

First, **emotional self-awareness**. I can't be assertive effectively if I'm not able to tap into what my feelings and beliefs are about things. My ability to separate out what I think and feel allows me to differentiate others from myself and determine what our relationship can be like. Even to understand the emotional range that other people are experiencing, to connect, to offer empathy requires as a foundation - an ability to know my own emotions.

Increasing emotional self-awareness is aided by exposure to the concepts of what the emotional options are. Again I reference Marc Brackett's work and his book *Permission to Feel.* In addition to offering us a brilliant model, the covers of his book include an emotions chart that can be life-changing for some coachees.

Pausing to check-in with yourself once or twice per day is a fantastic practice to increase emotional self-awareness. For some of us our body may give us the first clue about what is happening emotionally. 'Gee, my shoulders are up around my neck, I guess I'm tense about something.' Perhaps it's a change in heart rate or feeling butterflies in your stomach. Practicing taking what you notice and then working it back to get to deeper levels of emotional awareness is very helpful..

For instance, my shoulders are really tense. I've been working without a break. I feel nervous about getting everything done on my list this morning. I'm worried about disappointing my boss if I don't get this report to her by 3 pm. I feel inadequate and like I don't have enough to contribute on this topic. I feel some shame and I think that's an old story. I am feeling alone in doing this.

Second, **self-regard**. In order to function effectively in all of the other areas of EQ healthy self-regard matters. When my ability to respect me, prioritize my needs and offer myself compassion is compromised it impacts how well I can genuinely connect. It affects stress management, good decision making, how independently I can function etc. I would argue that every other aspect of emotional intelligence is impacted by self-regard and can be positively impacted by growth in this one area.

There are no quick tricks to get better at self-regard. So much of the way we view ourselves gets established pretty early in our lives. A wonderful resource on this topic is Dr. Kristin Neff who really pushes us to grow here through the perspective of self-compassion. Self-regard is not about feeling better about yourself because you are smarter or funnier or prettier than someone else. It is truly about really coming to terms with your incredible worth and value - period. It is Dr. Brené Brown's 'worthy of love and belonging' thinking.

In my experience for myself and with coachees there needs to be some core thinking changes to allow for the behavioral and emotional changes that are also critical for higher self-regard. This is the topic of much of our work as coaches. As thinking partners with our clients we can look at the limiting beliefs about self and self-regard and begin the journey towards a healthy self-acceptance and compassion for self.

I'd love to leave you with a few more reflection questions. We are coaches after all!

What are your top three emotional intelligence strengths that benefit your coaching clients regularly?

To continue to increase your understanding of this important topic, what will you do next?

Who models an area of emotional intelligence that you'd like to focus on growing? How can you learn from them?

Bio

Marilyn Orr has been coaching since 2005 supporting executives, entrepreneurs, students and fellow coaches in Canada and the USA. Marilyn is a mentor coach and loves helping coaches as they pursue credentials and ongoing development.

Speaking and training has been part of Marilyn's career for 25 years. Recent topics include emotional intelligence, leadership and coaching competencies - e.g. Emotional Intelligence and Conflict and Assertiveness + Empathy: Underutilized and Misunderstood. In 2019 Marilyn became a Training Partner with Multi-Health Systems, the developer of the EQ-i 2.0 assessment tool. She certifies professionals in correctly interpreting and using this emotional intelligence tool.

Marilyn believes that emotional intelligence growth is a big part of both resilience and leadership. Her extroverted personality comes out to play both one-on-one and with groups wanting to grow their skills. Clients report no judgment and laughing lots.

Recently she and her husband completed the creation of The Cedars Ranch, a sustainable event center focused on wellness. If you'd like to reach out to Marilyn for coaching around emotional intelligence, leadership or resilience feel free to visit her webpage.

https://www.capacitybc.com

EMOTION COACHING FOR HIGHER IMPACT

By Elly van Laar, ACC

Emotion Coaching for Higher Impact

You might be a life coach, business coach or leadership coach. Maybe you are a therapist with a curiosity about working with feelings in your sessions or you are just interested in the topic of emotion coaching and how it can help your relationships.

Whatever your motivation, at the end of this chapter you will have some insights to help you to acknowledge, accept, understand and use feelings in a kind and constructive way. May this chapter nurture loving-kindness toward yourself and others!

Here are some of the topics you will read about:

- What check-engine lights can tell you about feelings and needs

- How turning away from feelings diminishes your client's trust in you

- Why coaches might be interested in the "Love Lab"

- What pseudo-feelings are and why you

should care about them

What the journey of Frodo and Sam can teach us about sympathetic triggers

Your client has strong feelings, now what?

It's Tuesday morning and you just poured your first coffee. You open your Zoom account to start your eighth session with Marie. She is the fundraiser for a nonprofit dedicated to racial equity. As soon as she joins the session, she bursts out: "My boss is so aggressive! He interrupts everyone during the meetings. I feel disrespected and bullied into doing things I don't want to do."
Do you let her blow off steam in the first few minutes then re-direct the focus back to the goals she said she wanted to accomplish?

Maybe you're a divorce coach and your client is a father who fumes about being undermined by his ex-wife because she allows their daughter to spend hours on social media.

Are you sympathetically triggered because the situation reminds you of your ex-partner?

What about a client who says he is taken advantage of by his team member who "delegates the boring and hard work to him and then takes credit for it"?

Does his anger lessen your enthusiasm to dig into the issues?

All our clients come to their sessions with feelings. Sometimes we struggle with how to respond to them, especially when our clients have feelings we don't like having ourselves. That's why it helps to develop our emotional intelligence: the more we can accept and understand our own feelings, the more we can help our clients navigate their emotional whirlwinds.

Ignoring feelings creates cognitive strain

Your client's feelings don't get resolved by not acknowledging them. Your client might stop talking about them and try focusing on their stated coaching goals but the emotional charge still impacts their rational thinking.

Thich Nhat Hanh, a Vietnamese Buddhist teacher-monk, talks about holding our strong feelings as if they were a crying baby. No loving parent puts their crying baby in a closet, locks it up and walks away. Not only does that sound cruel but it also doesn't resolve the issue behind the crying. Sure, the baby eventually will stop crying, but the parent also has taught the baby to stop sending out any signals. Without those signals, we have less to coach on and we have missed the opportunity to deepen trust - trust that we meet our clients wherever they are at, that we have compassion for their emotional charge, and that we listen to their experiences with curiosity.

On the origin of our negativity bias

There is a good reason why it's hard to "get over" feelings. Anger, contempt, disgust, embarrassment, fear, guilt, sadness and shame are reactions to perceived threats to and loss of our emotional, social, physical or mental well-being. They are so ingrained in our brain that they trigger an immediate response. It's better to jump away from the rattlesnake than to spend a few seconds to see if it's a hose and then find out it *was* a rattlesnake.

Rick Hanson, a psychologist specializing in neuroplasticity, explains this negativity bias by going all the way back to the days on the Serengeti plains. Joe, a happy, positive guy, feels elated with the beautiful sunset when he peeks his head out of his hut. On his morning stroll on the plains, he gets so absorbed by the grace of the antelopes that he doesn't notice the leopard sneaking up on him. Bam! He ends up as breakfast and doesn't survive to pass his genes onto us.

Peter, his tribe member, is anxious, maybe even neurotic. He is constantly scanning his environment for potential danger. He does see the leopard behind him and has enough time to climb to safety in the acacia tree. The anxious guy does pass on his genes *and* his anxiety and obsession to look for the negative. That's why we have Velcro for the negative and Teflon for the positive.

Add to this negativity bias our unique human capacity to imagine our future and it's easy to understand that our amygdala can get activated just by thinking about a stressful event - even when there is no actual threat.

And since our brain likes coherence more than chaos, we weave these frightening scenarios into a story that makes sense to us. According to Daniel Kahneman, author of *Thinking Fast and Slow,* it is the coherence of these stories that tricks our brain into thinking they are true. Even though this coherence reduces cognitive strain, at the same time it reduces the ability of our prefrontal cortex to find creative solutions for our situation.

As coaches, we can help our clients to acknowledge their feelings, understand their negativity bias and help them evaluate the validity of their stories. We accept the emotional charge "as is" and invite the prefrontal cortex to get involved in next steps.

The best use of reality for creative tension

In *The Fifth Discipline,* Peter Senge writes about the tension between our reality and our vision. Most of us see room for improvement and wish our reality were at least a bit different. Maybe we want a more decluttered house, more financial safety, or a happier marriage.

When a vision seems impossible to reach, this discrepancy turns into emotional tension. We feel overwhelmed and lower our vision to match our reality.

When we trust there is a way forward, the discrepancy catalyzes creative tension. This is where coaches can play a powerful role. We can help our clients accept their feelings as part of their current reality. With this clarity they can craft a realistic path to move forward.

Picture a tourist who wants to visit the Taj Mahal. She hires a guide and they are ready to travel. Would they walk east without looking at the map? Of course not! If they're in Pakistan, going east makes sense. But if they are in Hokkaido going east would put them in the Pacific Ocean. Which direction you take depends as much on where you start as on where you are going.

Desmond Tutu writes in *The Book of Joy* how the acceptance of reality doesn't equal the inevitability of reality. If your client bangs their head against the pecan tree in the front yard, it helps them to accept that there is a tree instead of pretending it's not there. Once they accept that, they can choose whether they want to trim it, build a path around it or leave the house through the back door.

Coaches sometimes label emotional tension as resistance and defensiveness. I like how William R. Miller and Stephen Rollnick, the founders of Motivational Interviewing, reframe resistance and defensiveness as a combination of "sustain talk" and "discord". They both arise in our relationship with a client. What we might call resistance and defensiveness is actually a reflection of our inability to let them explore the needs underlying their feelings.

When we see and include feelings as part of the plan making, clients are better able to brainstorm how to deal with them. Some clients might choose smaller steps that are easier to achieve. Others might forge bold and audacious goals and make greater requests of themselves or others when these feelings arise. Both strategies will be successful when they engage reality.

Check-engine lights, feelings, and needs

As coaches, we can use feelings like we would use a check-engine light in our car. We don't cover our dashboard with duct tape because we don't know how to deal with the check engine light. We don't hit it with a hammer just because we are angry that it's broken.

No, we open the hood and see what needs attention. If we don't know anything about engines, we take our car to the mechanic and let her look at it. We use the check-engine light as a source of information. Feelings are a check-engine light for precious, universal human needs.

When our needs are met we have feelings that we like: glad, satisfied, peaceful, exhilarated, enthusiastic to name a few. When our needs are not met, we have feelings that we don't like: sadness, jealousy, disgust, anger, fear, contempt. Feelings are neither positive nor negative. They are messengers of needs like lights on a dashboard.

We share these needs throughout space and time. Marshall Rosenberg, the founder of Nonviolent Communication, listed 47 needs. Needs like acceptance, respect, rest, autonomy, celebration, community for example. You'll find them as an appendix to this chapter. Romans wanted respect just like we do. People in medieval Bologna wanted community and current-day Indigenous populations want that too. Homo Erectus wanted food and people in China too.

Life Pursuits

In *Authentic Happiness,* Martin Seligman distinguishes three life pursuits. The first is pursuing a happy life where we strive to have feelings that we like. It can be a feeling of awe when watching the Nederlands Dans Theater, or a sense of gratitude because your friend helps you during a move, or the delight you feel when your baby smiles at you.

In this realm, clients use their feelings to understand and fulfill their underlying needs. If your client is single and feels lonely, he might have an unmet need for closeness, love, and touch. He might commit to spending more energy in finding a partner. If your client lost her job and feels sad, she might have an unmet need for meaning and community. You could help her brainstorm how to look for a meaningful job in a community she likes. If your client struggles to bounce back from Covid and feels overwhelmed, there might be an unmet need for rest and support. In the session, you could work on which beliefs stop them from asking for help.

In an engaging life, clients seek experiences that bring them into flow. Martin Seligman writes:

"Engagement is about flow: being one with the music, time stopping, and the loss of self-consciousness during an absorbing activity. ... Engagement is different, even opposite, from positive emotion; for if you ask people who are in flow what they are thinking and feeling, they usually say, "nothing." In flow, we merge with the object. I believe that the concentrated attention that flow requires uses up all the cognitive and emotional resources that make up thought and feeling.

There are no shortcuts to flow. On the contrary, you need to deploy your highest strengths and talents to meet the world in flow."

These clients might look for moments where they found flow using their feelings as a thermometer. Feelings of deep satisfaction and contentment point to engaging activities. Feelings of boredom, frustration, and hopelessness do not.

A meaningful life is a life dedicated to a purpose beyond ourselves. This can be in service of God, community, environmental justice, a more inclusive society or whatever brings meaning to your client. In *Man's Search for Meaning*, Viktor Frankl gives humbling examples of people who never surrendered their values and dedication to service even while being tortured. People in search of meaning accept unpleasant feelings as long as they can live their highest purpose.

The more we become like a car mechanic trained to see feelings as messengers of needs, the more our clients can look at their inner workings with curiosity and use their findings to live their dreams, values and goals.

The emotional swamp

Have you read *The Two Towers,* the second volume in *The Lord of the Rings* trilogy by J.R.R. Tolkien? On their way to Mordor, Gollum leads Frodo and Sam through the "Mere of Dead Faces." He warns them not to touch the candle-like lights that appear to float over the marshes. Travelers who are hypnotized by these lights will touch the bodies and are likely to drown in the waters and join the dead. When Frodo gets mesmerized, Sam stops his trance and brings him back to their mission, the destruction of the one ring to rule them all.

While feelings are not dead faces, they can create an emotional swamp if we are sympathetically triggered because of similarities with our own experiences. Our sympathy distracts us from being present with our clients. We listen more to our thoughts or our emotional disquiet than to our clients' verbal and non-verbal signals. We might also suffer from a distracting inner Dr. Freud who leads us astray with analysis, judgments, interpretations or evaluations of our client's feelings.

There are at least two Sams to guide us through the swamp so we can coach clients with strong feelings.

Sam number 1

This Sam reminds us of Steven Hayes' concept of "cognitive defusion": realizing that having a feeling is not the same as being it. In our everyday language, we say things like "I am sad," "I am angry," and "I am scared" as though we are what we feel. Yet who we are is more than what we're feeling in each moment.

Hayes suggests more precise language: "I have a feeling of anger," or "I have a feeling of fear." This helps clients to see the full richness of themselves including but not limited to their feelings. If you find "I have a feeling of anger" a bit clumsy, you can help your client by replacing the "I am" with "I am feeling," creating a bit more space between who they are and what they are feeling.

Sam number 2

This Sam warns us about pseudo-feelings. Marshall Rosenberg describes these as feelings mixed with a thought about what someone else is doing to us. Pseudo-feelings often can be recognized by asking whether you can put "*by*" at the end of them. This signals the other-directedness. "I feel unsupported *by* my team," "I feel unappreciated *by* the CEO," or "I feel disrespected *by* the Board of Directors." You will find a list of the most common pseudo-feelings at the end of this chapter.

When we repeat pseudo-feelings back to our clients, we reinforce the implicit blame in them. As if we confirm that what others are saying or doing is the cause of our feelings, instead of the stimulus. Yes, other people's actions can be a stimulus. But the root cause is our needs and thoughts about the situation.

This is not to say that pseudo-feelings should be dismissed. The judgments, evaluations, interpretations, and emotional baggage that show up as pseudo-feelings offer a wonderful opportunity to explore the observations, feelings, thoughts, and needs hidden in them.

For example, Joan feels interrupted by Mike in the meeting. She stuttered as a child and had a talkative and funny older funny sibling who talked over her. Even though she doesn't stutter anymore and is quite verbal herself, she is still sensitive about having enough space to talk. Interrupted might be a shortcut for feeling anxious or frustrated. She might be anxious to receive appreciation that her ideas are useful or frustrated if she wants respect for her contribution.

When you ask Joan to describe what happened as factual as possible, she might tell you that she talked for ten seconds and then

Mike talked at the same time and everyone's attention turned to him.

Drawing out observations makes it easier to imagine other interpretations. Maybe Mike comes from a culture where it's considered polite to talk as soon as there is silence to show that you're engaged in the conversation. It could be that Mike had no ill intent: he just got excited about Joan's idea and wanted to add to it.

This more factual observation can help your client redirect their attention to their feelings and needs, instead of finding fault with Mike. It allows for brainstorming strategies to meet those needs. Maybe Joan wants to tell Mike about her experience or she might want to email her contribution to the team before the meeting.

Turning Towards

In 1986, John Gottman and Robert Levenson built an apartment laboratory at the University of Washington that was dubbed the "Love Lab" by the media. Over many decades they observed thousands of couples and noted their facial expressions, heart rates, blood pressure, skin conductivity and the words they used in conversation with their partners.

They found that couples that stayed married turned towards each other's bids for emotional connection 86% of the time. Couples that divorced averaged only 33% of the time.

Zach Brittle writes on the Gottman blog:

"A bid is any attempt from one partner to another for attention, affirmation, affection or any other positive connection. Bids show up in simple ways, a smile or wink and more complex ways like a request for advice or help. In general, women make more bids than me but in the healthiest relationships, both partners are comfortable making all kinds of bids.

To "miss" a bid is to "turn away." Turning away can be devastating. It's even more devastating than "turning against" or rejecting the bid. Rejecting a bid at least provides the opportunity for continued engagement and repair. Missing the bid results in diminished bids, or worse, making bids for attention, enjoyment and affection somewhere else."

Imagine your client comes into the session, sits down and sighs deeply. In Gottman's model, the sigh is the bid for emotional connection. Turning against this would be something like "Geez, man, what's wrong with you today?" Since we see our clients as whole, creative and resourceful, contempt or criticism are not part of our tool bag.

We might be turning away however. Most turning away isn't intentional. We might miss the sigh, facial expression or tone of voice. A lot is going on in a session and we only can pay attention to a limited number of cues. We want to add value and help our clients move forward but perhaps we listen more to the words than to the nonverbal cues. Even though acknowledging the non-verbal cues builds trust and signals engagement.

Turning toward can be as simple as "That's a sigh," or "It sounds frustrating," or "There is a lot of energy when you say that." Your client immediately knows that you value their whole being, not just what they're saying.

Once you hear their response to your turning toward, you can ask how they want to proceed. Some feel uncomfortable talking about their feelings. It might feel to them like they are being undressed while you keep your coat on. They might be satisfied with your acknowledgment, then work on their goals and aspirations. Other clients need more empathy before they can focus on a larger goal. It might help them to explore the observations, needs and requests that are associated with those feelings.

In *Hold Me Tight,* Sue Johnson describes how "effective dependency... to turn to others for emotional support is a sign and source of strength." As coaches, we can offer that emotional support and help our clients trust that what they share matters. When you stay emotionally attuned to your client, you can help them get from where they are right now to where they want to be. You coach them on what's most meaningful to them.

What's next?

This is a great moment to write down three "aha" moments and how those moments can help you move yourself and others forward.

- Was it that our brain has a negativity bias - Rick Hanson's Teflon and Velcro analogy for negative events?

- Is it the idea of creative tension - that we need to accept our current reality, feelings and all, to get closer to our vision?

- Maybe you got inspired by feelings as the check-engine light for needs - precious, human, universal needs that we share throughout space and time.

- Is it that you like to reflect more on the happy, engaging or meaningful life?

- It can also be that you liked the reminder of cognitive defusion and wonder how you can have your feelings without identifying with them.

- You might never have heard of pseudo-feelings and are committed to reading more about how mixing thoughts, feelings and needs in one word can contribute to enemy images.

- You might be excited to learn more about the "Love Lab" and turn toward others more often.

Perhaps you are the lucky one who didn't gain any new insight! Then thank you so much for sticking with me till the end. I hope you share your insights with me, so I can learn from you!

Whatever you're walking away with, I would love to read your response! There is no chapter without an audienc super grateful that you stayed with me. I answer a though sometimes my response may be a bit slow.

Precious, human, universal needs

Autonomy
- To choose one's dreams, goals, values
- To choose one's plan for fulfilling one's dreams, goals, values

Celebration
- To celebrate the creation of life and dreams fulfilled
- To celebrate losses: loved ones, dreams (mourning)

Integrity
- Authenticity
- Creativity
- Meaning
- Self-Worth

Interdependence
- Acceptance
- Appreciation
- Closeness
- Community
- Consideration
- Contribution
- Emotional Safety
- Empathy
- Honesty
- Love
- Reassurance
- Respect
- Support
- Trust
- Understanding
- Warmth

Play
- Fun
- Laughter

Spiritual Communion
- Beauty
- Harmony
- Inspiration
- Order
- Peace

Physical Nurturance
- Air
- Food
- Movement, exercise
- Protection
- Rest
- Shelter
- Touch
- Water

Common pseudo-feelings

Abandoned	Harassed	Put down
Abused	Ignored	Rejected
Attacked	Insulted	Taken for granted
Belittled	Interrupted	Threatened
Betrayed	Intimidated	Tricked
Blamed	Invalidated	Unappreciated
Boxed-in	Invisible	Unheard
Bullied	Isolated	Unseen
Cheated	Left out	Unsupported
Coerced	Let down	Unwanted

Co-opted	Manipulated	Used
Cornered	Misunderstood	Victimized
Criticized	Neglected	Violated
Diminished	Overworked	
Discounted	Patronized	
Disrespected	Pressured	
Distrusted	Provoked	

Bio

Elly van Laar specializes in leadership development and conflict coaching for nonprofit leaders. She is a recognized expert in Nonviolent Communication, conflict resolution, and self-compassion.

Over the past 24 years, Elly has worked in and with nonprofits. She has been a frontline worker, Director of Programming, and Board member of the Austin Mediators Association and the local chapter of the International Coach Federation.

In addition, Elly is a frequent speaker on empathy, emotional regulation, and conflict resolution. She belongs to Thich Nhat Hanh's mindfulness community, volunteers at the Austin Dispute Resolution Center, and offers meditation classes in jail.

And if she is not coaching or mediating? Then you can find her on her meditation cushion, visiting friends and family in the Netherlands, or juggling. And, hanging out with her fan and teacher, her husband David Nayer.

To find out more about Elly visit www.ellyvanlaar.com.

PROBING PERSONALITIES PROVIDES POSSIBILITIES

By Edna Harris, BA, MA, PCC

I recently shared with a friend that I would be writing about personality assessments. Her response was, "You better be ready to write a book!" She was right. Within minutes of beginning my research, I had located over 50 assessments.

The intention of this article is NOT to describe all 50+ assessments but to:

- define/describe Personality Assessments (PAs),

- provide an overview of the DiSC, an example of one PA,

- state the benefits of using PAs for the coach personally,

- share how PA's serve as a tool to inform the coach/client interaction, and

- describe some strategies for integrating PAs into a coaching practice.

First, personality assessments are designed to be a quantitative measurement of personal characteristics or traits. These indicators impact decision-making, thinking, perceiving, learning and emotions. These instruments describe the way we show up in the world and the actions we take since an individual's personality is linked to socially significant aspects of behavior. Although personalities really do not change over time, our behaviors or how we interact with others can. PAs can help people understand their strengths and challenges, identify career matches, specify what drains/energizes them, explain why they get along with some people and not others and pinpoint a person's leadership skills.

Second, personality assessments vary in many ways. Some of these differences include:

1. the specific personality characteristics they reveal,

2. the number of personal characteristics they identify,

3. cost,

4. the time it takes to complete the test, and

5. the number of additional, specialized assessments and services available from the company.

I prefer the DiSC personality assessment. The initials in DiSC are an acronym that correspond to the four basic personalities identified in the assessment.

D stands for DOMINANCE. Ds are direct, results-oriented, firm, strong-willed, forceful (3% of the population)

I stands for INFLUENCE. Is are outgoing, enthusiastic, optimistic, high-spirited, lively (11% of population)

S stands for STEADINESS. Ss are even-tempered, accommodating, patient, humble, tactful (69% of population)

C stands for CONSCIENTIOUSNESS. Cs are analytical, reserved, precise, private, systematic (17% of population)

Although individuals tend to score higher in one or two of these dimensions, their behavior is influenced by scores in all domains; therefore, how these behaviors interact are unique for each person. I find that people can easily understand the interplay among these four personality characteristics; hence, they are able to retain and apply the data over time. There are free DiSC tests available and initial assessments can be completed in 7-10 minutes. Once individuals complete this first assessment, there are many additional in-depth instruments available for a fee. My DiSC preference is also based on the fact that I was originally exposed to DiSC and am a certified trainer in that system. The DiSC is also commonly used with teams to help team members see how others process information and solve problems. These insights then lead to better communication among the members of the team.

Since personality assessments differ in the way they report an individual's data, they generally provide some broad interpretation markers. The DiSC uses two sets of markers that are recorded as continuums. First, people are generally task oriented (Ds, Cs) or people oriented (Is, Ss); secondly, they are active (Ds, Is) or passive (Ss, Cs) in their thinking and responses. PAs then use words to describe the more specific behaviors of various groups of people.

Third, it is helpful if coaches know what their personality style reveals about themselves and how that knowledge might impact their interaction with a client. On the DiSC, I am an I/S. I tend to favor people over tasks, to see the big picture and not details, to take words at face value, and to process data and move quickly. My challenge in my coaching role becomes to probe my clients for details in the actions they plan to take and to slow down the pace of my language. When coaching an "S", I might say, "You said you want to have a conversation with your boss. Let me give you a minute to think about what you want to say during that conversation. [pause]. When will that conversation take place? Where? Would it be helpful to role play that inter-action?" I also want to explore what clients mean by the words they use. For example, when coaching any of the DiSC behavior characteristics, I might say "What does 'stuck' mean to you? Where does that definition come from for you?" I believe under-standing my personality style and how I interact with others en-hances my effectiveness as a coach.

One of the ways I continue to grow as a coach is to take additional PAs. I recently completed the Enneagram and learned that I was a type 7—an enthusiastic visionary. The words used to describe this type correspond to the behavior characteristics I learned about myself on the DiSC. I also learned that I am a "thinker". Thinkers are problem solvers. This reminded me that my role as a coach is not to solve my client's issues or give advice but to simply offer non-judgmental possibilities.

Fourth, understanding my client's personality style contrib-utes to a successful interaction between the coach and client. Often, clients initially contract with a coach for a limited num-ber of sessions i.e., twice a month for three months or 6 sessions; therefore, coaches want to establish a close, intimate client re-lationship quickly. When successful, this dialogue often results in clients sharing their frustrations, fears and disappointments. Daniel Kahneman in *Thinking Fast and Slow* says when emo-tions are involved in any interaction, people tend to resist self-exploration. "We need someone outside our head to disrupt our thinking by listening to us, reflecting back our thinking and then asking questions that prompt us to wonder why we think the way we do," states Marcia Reynolds in *Breakthrough Coaching*. PAs provide a process for coaches to create a safe place for this coach-client relationship to emerge in a short amount of time.

Here are some examples of how I have used my knowledge of DiSC personality styles to guide my coaching interactions.

Coaching a "C"

After I had been coaching for about five years, I was required to complete a case study as part of an advanced coaching certification; consequently, I have the most notes from that coaching interaction. I will refer to this client as MB. At that time, she was an assistant principal and told me that she had been a science teacher. She shared that she chose that profession because she was a concrete, systematic thinker. Even though MB had not completed a DiSC assessment, I quickly learned that she was analytical and data driven. She preferred to find answers and solutions in books or on the internet and needed a lot of information before she was ready to make a decision. MB struggled to ask other people for their assistance. Based on these descriptors, I determined that she was a "C".

MB also shared that she worked with a principal who was right-brained, saw big pictures, was social, and was not detailed-oriented (probably an "I"). Since MB was responsible for discipline on her campus, she struggled with the differences between her role and that of the counselors. Together we developed plans to clarify her role and those of her principal, the counselors and the office staff. MB developed a flow chart, then a Venn Diagram reflecting these roles and vowed to have honest, open conversations with the counseling staff. One of her goals was to expand her problem-solving abilities to include paying attention to her gut feelings and to listen for what had heart for her and for others. One of her strategies became seeking insights, knowledge and assistance from people and not just relying on information obtained from researching answers from experts in printed materials. MB realized that she needed this knowledge if she was to be seen as a team player and a contributing member of her school and district, skills she valued.

Some things came easy for MB—developing a bullying program for her school, writing articles for the campus newsletter, collecting research around a variety of topics, creating an assistant principal's handbook. These tasks represented a big part of her skillset as an administrator. Since these abilities were second nature to her, she often only mentioned these accomplishments briefly during our time together. MB never completed the celebration question on her prep form. As a strategy to change her mind set about the value of her contributions, I wanted to help her not only recognize tasks she could celebrate as part of her every-day accomplishments but to help her explore ways to celebrate. As an "I" coach, it never occurred to me that some sort of recognition or celebration was not a part of every person's repertoire at some level.

I also learned the importance of having the client complete the prep form. During our last session together, I asked MB's permission to share an observation with her about the number of times and the content of situations she had shared regarding her relationship with her principal. This was a theme that ran through every one of our interactions. She gave her permission. After considering the data I provided and giving my observation some thought, MB agreed that this interaction was an important part of her life and it was not as good as she wanted it to be. We then developed a plan of action designed to enhance her relationship with her principal. As her coach, I felt we were focused and went deeper into dealing with a real issue facing her during this session. At the end of the session, she indicated that we had not talked about the issue she had listed on her prep form. Upon reflection, I came to realize that MB might have been using the prep form to unconsciously keep me from asking her the harder questions. I became acutely aware as a coach that when I choose to surface hidden behaviors, no matter how strong the intimate, trusting relationship is between my client and me, I run the risk of frightening the client away. I suspect this may have happened with MB. Asking her to take responsibility for her behavior with her principal—to develop a different relationship —may have been more than she could handle as she terminated our relationship.

Although I feel as though MB benefited from our coaching sessions, there may have been any number of reasons she chose not to continue. When I reviewed my coaching notes, I realized that she did not deal with confrontation at any level of complexity. During one session, MB shared how disappointed she was in the behavior of one of the teachers who had planned a going away party for one of the office staff and chose not to invite the principal. MB decided not to go to the party because she felt as though she needed to support her principal. Although MB was upset, she elected not to have an honest conversation with the teacher. When the staff sent a letter to the superintendent complaining about their principal, rather than tell the staff that she didn't support their decision, she chose to walk away if conversations developed around this topic. Although I lost MB as a client, as her coach I felt it was my moral obligation to surface behaviors that might be keeping her from obtaining her goals in life. I felt as though I presented this observation with data and in a loving, caring manner with a supportive tone of voice. This situation has made my role as a coach clearer to me and I would not change my decision to share this information with MB even though she chose to end the relationship.

Other factors perhaps clouded this relationship. MB was assigned to me as part of a contract with my coaching company. I am also aware that clients who do not pay directly for their coaching services (MB's district paid for her to receive coaching), may not be as committed to the process as those who contract directly with the coach. During our coaching sessions, MB shared that her principal had completed training with my coaching company and as part of that training, she had received coaching. Thus, the principal wanted MB to be coached. I felt as though MB was not committed to the coaching process. Perhaps she only agreed to participate because it was her principal's request or the principal may have made coaching a requirement for MB's professional growth. Her behavior reinforced this lack of commitment as she often showed up late for our calls or canceled sessions and had excuses for why she had not accomplished what she created during our time together.

Since MB elected not to have an exit interview, I will never know what she felt she gained from the coaching process. I can only speculate about what she learned. I used a variety of strategies to help MB deal with issues—paraphrasing, reframing, linking current behavior/situation to her long-term goals, silence, questioning, asking about feelings, giving her agenda choices, exploring alternative perspectives, surfacing assumptions/patterns, asking for or providing examples to test assumptions, etc. Of these, I feel as though questioning, paraphrasing, reframing and exploring alternative perspectives seemed to assist MB with her thinking the most. By not encouraging complaining about her principal's behaviors, I was able to help her focus on what she was learning about her own leadership style based upon the behaviors she observed in her principal. She came to embrace the learning opportunities that her principal provided—conferences, serving on committees, presenting at a board meeting—to see them as opportunities to grow in her understanding of the principal's role and not as additional duties. By changing her perspective regarding these projects, MB moved out of using victim language and was able to become more empowered to take the initiative. She embraced Covey's concept of Sphere of Influence stating, "I don't have to be a principal to do principal-like things."

She took on some district wide projects—leading the district character development program, working with the staff at Central Office to update the district website, sharing the policy/procedures manual she had developed for her role as an assistant principal and using some teachers on her campus to help her implement the bullying program. I was able to suggest that some of the same qualities she admired in her principal i.e., being sociable and charming were also within her skillset but that since her leadership style was different, these qualities would be exhibited in another manner. MB realized that her leadership style must emerge from her own value system of inclusiveness. Even though she felt more comfortable researching issues and developing possible solutions from experts in the field, she also desired team work and participatory interaction. MB was able to label her leadership style as servant leadership and saw her role as contributing, participatory.

Although I am not sure what MB would say she gained from coaching, she spoke highly of the experience to other administrators in her district and they in turn sought coaching services. I wonder how she explained the coaching process since I could not totally lose the feeling that she never used the process to alter her life in any significant way. Coaching appeared to be the way she could talk about issues, get clearer about her thinking but only make small changes in her behavior. This coaching interaction made me realize how difficult change can be. Because Cs are private people, perhaps the changes MB made were as much as she was able to make at that point in her life.

Lessons I learned from this client:

1. It is possible to determine a client's personality style based upon their behaviors. Although it is helpful to have PA data, it is not necessary.

2. The prep form may be used by my client to keep the conversation from going deeper. I now ask myself if the client and I need to be having the conversation on the prep form or a deeper conversation that I can suggest around themes, patterns, hidden agendas that will surface behaviors that may be hidden from my clients.

3. It is difficult to coach someone who is not totally committed to trusting the process—who may not be ready to reveal deeper thoughts and emotions or someone who is being coached to please the requirements of their boss.

4. As a coach, I cannot want more for my client than they are willing to want for themselves. I have to practice "letting go".

Coaching a "D/I"

I recently agreed to present the DiSC assessment

When you think of resiliency what comes to mind? Let's consider both some visuals and a few definitions.

A metal spring is the image that represents resiliency to me. It can be compressed or stretched and returns back to its shape. I also have the assessment at my friend Jane's workshop on leadership. Although she provided me with basic information—date, amount of time I would have to share my content—I was not actively involved in the agenda nor the logistics. The training session had many excellent presenters and great, fun activities (Is always plan for fun!). Even though the workshop evaluations indicated that the session was a success, it lost a considerable amount of money! After the session was over, Jane asked for a coaching session as she was unsure why this happened. As we explored the possibilities, it became apparent that since she was developing a new company, she had surrounded herself with visionaries and dreamers (Ds/Is). No one on the team served as a financial advisor tracking the monies collected for registration nor the monies spent on program booklets and planning documents for the participants (C). There was also no individual who put processes in place to get the work done in an efficient, organized way (S). My friend was a D/I who was attempting to do all these tasks herself or relying on other Ds/Is to assist her. Recognizing that the skills needed to explore business options/possibilities were not the same as those needed to organize and present a profitable workshop, Jane stated that she definitely needed to hire an "S/C" administrative assistant and would use the DiSC personality assessment as a part of hiring this individual.

Coaching a "S"

There is a good reason why 69% of the population are S's. We need them to help the rest of us organize and figure out how to get work done. Meet my client Sally. She worked as the administrative assistant to an area superintendent of a large suburban school district. She fielded questions from every part of the organization—parents, teachers, principals, school board members, community leader, central office staff. She was responsible for conveying information to and from her boss to these individuals and the superintendent. As the oldest of five children, she has taken responsibility for the care of her mother who was in the hospital and she was trying to emotionally support her youngest daughter who was going through a divorce and had moved back home.

During our coaching sessions, Sally expressed feelings of being tired, frustrated and overwhelmed. She was great at putting processes in place but often didn't know what order important tasks needed to be done. As we worked together, Sally developed strategies for setting priorities i.e., asking her boss to help her decide what to do first. We developed language like, "Here is a list of everything I need to do. What do you see as the most important?" or "As we plan today, what is it you want me to be sure to complete before the end of the day?" We created categories for her work like: "What I like to do;" "Tasks I can hand off to someone else to help them develop new skills;" "Tasks I can decline or postpone." We talked about how to say No when appropriate, how to make "I" statements instead of "you" statements, how to set boundaries and the difference between a request and a demand.

As our sessions progressed, Sally found her voice. She discovered that she could set up a schedule when she would be available to her mom, her siblings and her daughter instead of constantly responding to their every need 24 hours a day. We practiced how she would communicate that request to her family members. As a result of our coaching, Sally asked for what she wanted, took control of her life and was surprised she was able to do this without making anyone angry. She stated she felt empowered, was getting more accomplished at home and at work and was sleeping better at night.

In each of these stories, coaching made a difference in the life of the client. Understanding the personality styles of my clients helped me establish a trusting relationship with each of them in a short period of time and I used the information to set direction for our coaching sessions. So, as a coach, how will you obtain PA data from your clients?

Here are some possibilities:

- Ask your clients if they have ever completed a PA. Many businesses, churches and organizations use them in their hiring practice or as part of team building activities. If they have, explore what they learned about themselves. "How does this data shape how you show up at work? At home? In a new situation?" This conversation may take the form of a verbal interview during a pre-hire session or this investigation may be part of the information you request from clients in your welcome packet or as part of your initial signed contract with your client.

- If your clients have never completed an assessment, ask them to take one. Many companies offer free or low-cost options. (See suggestions listed on the resource page.)

After the coach is in a coaching relationship with a client, here are some ways to continue to use their personality style:

- Hold the client's strengths/challenges as a thread that runs through your coaching interactions. For a client who focusses on tasks and has set a goal to be more people focused ("D"), the coach might say, "One of your strengths has been to hold a clear vision toward a specific goal. What are you doing to keep this goal visible to others? What strategies have you put in place that let you know that others are with you?" or "As you work on bringing others along with you, how are you assessing where they are?"

- Another interaction with this same client might sound like, "You stated that you wanted to develop your people skills. What help are you requesting from me?" "How do you want me to hold you accountable for reaching this goal?"

Within a few months after the coaching relationship has ended, follow-up with clients to see how they are continuing to implement the new mindset and strategies they developed as a result of the coaching sessions. This can be a text, email or a personal phone call. The communication can simply be a reminder of the improvement behaviors the clients set as goals around their PA or it can be reflected in a survey created by you to gather feedback regarding the effectiveness of your coaching skills. Clients appreciate knowing that their coach still thinks about them and continues to hold them in positive regard even when the coaching sessions have ended.

In summary, coaching interactions are designed to uncover new insights about how clients interact in the world and to explore possibilities for their growth/change. Coaches have the incredible opportunity to participate in this personal transformation. PAs like the DiSC are a powerful tool that can guide this evolution. When coaches add PAs to their coaching skill set, they grow in their understanding of their own behaviors and those of their clients. Using strategies to integrate personality assessments into a coaching practice enables coaching conversations to become impactful and dynamic thereby creating changes in the client's behaviors and positively enhancing their lives. How do you plan to incorporate personality assessments into your coaching repertoire?

References

Kahnemar, Daniel. *Thinking Fast and Slow*, 2011

Reynolds, .*Breakthrough Coaching*, 2021

Resources

Here are a few internet sites that offer free personality assessments:

a. Truity.com Established in 2012, Truity has developed
a library of scientifically validated personality tests to
help people understand themselves and those around
them. Range of tests include Enneagram, Typefinder,
and Workplace DiSC

b. Cloverleaf.com—DiSC, Strengthfinders, Enneagram. I
used this site to complete my Enneagram and now receive daily action tips on my type 7 profile.

c. 123test.com—Since 2003, 123test has been developing and
automating psychometric tests for all kinds of purposes—
primarily for individuals. Big 5 Personality Traits, DiSC

d. Mydiscprofile.com—DiSC

Bio

*From a young age, I knew I wanted to teach. When my brother was
diagnosed with a learning disability, I became intrigued with how
people learn which led me to seek my Master's degree in special
education. This learning/teaching desire guided me as I worked as
a teacher, Director of Staff Development for a large suburban school
district and as I pursued certification in a variety of programs like
leadership coaching, the DiSC personality assessment and as a Ther-
apon counselor.*

*Creating curriculum and developing training programs gives me
an intellectual high. My ability to see big concept pictures and
sequence the steps needed to present and master ideas helps me
develop graphics/mental models so concepts can be easily taught
and retained. Recently, I enjoyed developing customized Master-*

Mind processes for two separate organizations.

Currently, this teaching/learning passion has taken on another focus. After several mission trips to third world countries, I am now serving as a host to my second international college student from Haiti. These students bring me great joy and sometimes late nights as they allow me to be their mentor, tutor, coach and their American mom. They support and reinforce my love to work with individuals and groups to help them unlock their brilliance. I believe that when people know and stand on their values and beliefs, they are equipped to navigate the world and take effective actions that are grounded in their true identity and purpose.

SIGNATURE STRENGTHS, HAN SOLO AND THE GOLDEN MEAN

By Michelle M. Lopez, PhD, PCC, CEC

"Which Flat Solo will remind you of the strength you will bring to tomorrow's conversation with your team?"

"Well," Sam replied, "I'm going with Bravery."

"What does Bravery look and sound like tomorrow?"

Sam thought for a moment and answered confidently, "It's my confident self, seated at the table with my team, confronting the adversity that will be present during this difficult conversation and remaining authentic to myself as I address their concerns and complaints."

My client sorted through his deck of Flat Solos. The idea of using these "cards" came about during one of our first sessions as we discussed the various personality traits of Han Solo and how they could be used to bring out his own character strengths. Sam recalled The Flat Stanley Project which was initiated in

1995 by a third grade Canadian school teacher, Dale Hubert, based on the book by the same title. Stanley Lambchop is the main character of the book. He was accidentally flattened by a falling bulletin board, rolled up by his parents and mailed to his friend in California. Mr. Hubert thought this was a great way to encourage reading and writing among his students as they were all provided a cutout of Stanley, instructed to color it in, write a story about Flat Stanley and mail it to a friend. Flat Stanleys have appeared all over the world. I wonder if Mr. Hubert could have imagined that decades later his Flat Stanley Project would spark the idea of creating Flat Solos.

Returning to Sam, he sorted through his deck of Flat Solos and landed on the one with Han Solo looking cool, calm and collected, the embodiment of how he wanted to employ his strength of Courage. As a fan of Star Wars, Sam had identified the character of Han Solo as the image of the strong leader he wanted to embody during this phase of his career. He had created a deck of Han Solos for work and one for home. Sam referenced them throughout the week as reminders of his character strengths: Bravery, Perseverance, Kindness, Honesty and Humor.

As a coach, the opening vignette is one of the many unique ways my clients have integrated their character strengths into creating greater awareness of who they are being in the moment and who they would like to be in the future. This greater awareness results in identifying ways in which these strengths can be employed as they work toward their coaching goals. The strengths are derived from the VIA Character Strengths Survey.

Character Strengths and authentic happiness are considered the backbone of Positive Psychology. In 1998, Dr. Martin Seligman, serving as president of the American Psychological Association, addressed his colleagues by calling for the field of psychology to pivot its focus. Until that moment, psychologists had studied positive experiences but had given more weight to "problems" such as disorders, diseases, conflicts, than research on positive experiences. Dr. Seligman proposed positive psychology as the study of positive subjective experiences, positive traits and positive institutions. Since the beginning of the 21st century, research in positive psychology has grown exponentially.

One result of this change in focus was the creation of the 24 Character Strengths. Two of Positive Psychology's icons, Drs. Martin Seligman and Chris Peterson, participated with other notable scholars in the initial brainstorming of how to identify these strengths. Their guiding premise was to "leave no stone unturned" as they scoured text, cultural artifacts, works, core tenets, literature and programs on character. Each identified strength was tested against ten criteria. Of the 24 character strengths selected, all met at least nine of the criteria, except Zest and Love, which both met eight out of ten criteria. Those 24 character strengths are listed below, and may also be found online at the VIA Institute on Character homepage (viacharacter.org):Appreciation of Beauty & Excellence

- Bravery
- Creativity
- Curiosity
- Fairness
- Forgiveness
- Gratitude
- Honesty
- Hope
- Humility

- Humor
- Judgment
- Kindness
- Leadership
- Love
- Love of Learning
- Perseverance
- Perspective
- Prudence
- Self-Regulation
- Social Intelligence
- Spirituality
- Teamwork
- Zest

These 24 character strengths have been studied and have been found to be universal across 75 countries and resonate cross-culturally meaning they resonate with more than just the Western culture. According to the VIA Institute on Character, there are over 400 scientific publications written on the VIA Classification and every 15 seconds someone takes the free VIA Survey online. The results of the VIA Survey create a "common language" of strengths describing what is best in human beings.

So, what is a character strength? How does it differ from a talent or a skill? The following definitions are found in Dr. Ryan Niemiec's book, *Character Strengths Interventions: A Field Guide for Practitioners*. In addition to character strengths, there are other types of "strengths": *Talents, Skills, Interests, Resources* and *Values*.

Each type of strength has a unique definition. *Talents* are what we do naturally well. *Skills* are what we train ourselves to do. The strength of *Interests* is linked to our passions. The strength of *Resources* are our external support systems. *Values* are what we internally hold dear in our thoughts and emotions. The 24 character strengths intimately connect with each of these other strengths serving as a catalyst for the individual's self-awareness and utilization of a character strength. As written in *Character Strengths Interventions*, "In summary, talents can be squandered, resources can be quickly lost, interests wane and change, skills diminish over time, but when all seems completely lost, we still have our character strengths ... our character strengths crystallize and evolve and can integrate with these other positive qualities to contribute to the greater good." (Appendix A)

For my clients, their awareness of the 24 character strengths, particularly those that are ranked as their top five (Signature Strengths) is an integral part of their coaching experience. The Signature Strengths are ranked as the top five because they are *essential, energizing and effortless*. These top five strengths have become integral to my clients' understanding of their positive traits and how to cultivate and celebrate them. While two people might share the same ranked list of strengths, they will not embody these strengths in the same way. Each strength is uniquely employed by each person, almost like a unique strengths "fingerprint" and these character strengths help us understand our "being" (who we are) and our "doing" (behavioral expression).

I recall one young woman who graduated after the first few months of the global pandemic and decided to delay a job search hoping that the job market for new college graduates would improve. A few months after graduation, Laura came to coaching to assist her with a better understanding of her strengths and how they could be used to enter the workforce in a job that would be personally and professionally satisfying and fulfilling. Her Signature Strengths were: Love of Learning, Kindness, Humility, Fairness and Perspective. Taking the VIA Survey was the first opportunity Laura had been provided a list of her strengths. It was so new to her; she was not sure what to do with this wealth of information.

We spent one session reviewing the various types of strengths and how her character strengths were catalysts to working in tandem with one or more of her other types of strengths (e.g. talents, skills, values). As a homework inquiry, she spent that week writing about a time when she was at her best. We reviewed her story at the next session and we both engaged in strength spotting – we identified which of her Signature Strengths we "spotted" in memory of being at her best. What I recall from this conversation is that while Laura's top strength was Love of Learning, she was underutilizing this strength in exploring career options and her Humility was overused in that she was experiencing a limited self-image.

As these two strengths were out of balance, they were contributing to her lack of motivation and direction. We needed to bring these two strengths back into balance, or optimal use, so that she could combine these character strengths to the right degree and in the right situation. Discovering the optimal use of a strength is referred to as the Golden Mean. To use her Love of Learning more, she investigated job postings that appealed to her. Bringing these job descriptions to a session, we reviewed them looking for job duties that matched each of her strengths and how she would use that strength to address that job duty.

While this exercise required a lot of discussion and self-awareness, the deep dive into her strengths as they related to the job descriptions paid off for Laura. Once she revised her resume and wrote her general cover letter, she was employed soon after. The understanding of her strengths and how they can be overused and underused aided in her ability to demonstrate her character strengths as the Golden Mean.

Strength spotting can be achieved in a variety of ways. In addition to asking the client to reflect on a time when they were at their best, questions such as share a recent good experience at work, tell me about something positive in your life or what went well this week can also elicit opportunities to spot the client's strengths.

A character strength overused or underused is no longer a strength but an obstacle. Chasing the Golden Mean can facilitate rich discussion in a coaching session to explore relevant interventions or to reframe problems so that the client can see themselves from a different perspective. Note it is likely that overuse will occur in a top strength while underuse will occur in the lowest strengths. This strengths-blindness can be overcome when clients receive feedback and support from others including their coach.

As a matter of routine, I always have my client's top five strengths at hand during a session and reference them as often as relevant. A simple acknowledgment of the strength of kindness I have just observed from their description of how they responded to someone in need that week can evoke a smile of gratitude for noticing. Asking my client which strength might be holding them back from making progress toward their goal can foster discussion on how to find the Golden Mean of that strength. Or identifying the need to use a lesser strength that is being underused and asking the client to pair it with a Signature Strength can provide reinforcement for the client to make progress.

My coaching has been strongly influenced by using Character Strengths leading to innovative ways for my clients to use their strengths to support, encourage and challenge them in the "doing" and "being" of their lives. The quest for the Golden Mean is paramount. May this spark a way for you to help your clients create their own Han Solo intervention on their way to designing a life of happiness, fulfillment and wellbeing.

References

The Flat Stanley Project

https://en.wikipedia.org/wiki/The_Flat_Stanley_Project

VIA Institute

https://viacharacter.org

Niemiec, R. M. (2018). *Character Strengths Interventions: A Field Guide for Practitioners.*

Hogrefe Publishing Corporation: Boston, MA.

Bio

Michelle M. López is an ICF and EMCC credentialed professional coach, executive and team coach, coach trainer, educator and community leader. Professionally, she has held roles in higher education from faculty to student affairs administrator for over 25 years. Her experience led to the creation of her coaching and consulting company, Next Gen Latinos, LLC.

As a coach, she champions emerging and experienced leaders so that they achieve authentic action across their lives and live a great story! Her clients have included entrepreneurs, executive leaders, non-profit organizations, higher education administrators/teams and corporate teams. Clients characterize her coaching style as warm, encouraging, challenging, intuitive and collaborative. Her specialties include leadership development, values clarification, executive presence, personal branding, strategic planning and managing professional transitions.

Dr. López considers one of her proudest accomplishments as cultivating a vibrant marriage and family life for nearly 25 years that honors her values of faith, family, fun and authenticity.

RESILIENCY- BOUNCING BACK FROM CHANGE

By Teresa Bitner, PMP & M.ED., ACC

Resiliency and bouncing back from life's setbacks, isn't that what we all want?

Resiliency. What is it? What does it look like to you? What does it look like in your clients? Those are the questions we'll explore in this chapter. We'll begin with a couple of definitions to start with then examine how resiliency and change are intertwined. Through client vignettes we will explore resilient characteristics. Lastly, we'll review provocative, powerful questions to explore resiliency with your clients. I believe that with knowledge and intention everyone can build more resiliency. I also have the image of a tree growing from the side of a rock face standing strong. Using these two images we can begin to start our list of characteristics and define resiliency.

Here are a couple of dictionary definitions--"the ability to become strong, healthy, or successful again after a change happens." or "able to withstand or recover quickly from difficult conditions." https://www.merriam-webster.com/dictionary/resilience

Which resiliency definition or image resonates with you?

The last definition with the emphasis on withstanding is my personal favorite and what I see clients wanting to happen in their lives. The more tragic or uncomfortable the change the quicker they want to recover and bounce back.

Before we move into the examples of resiliency, let's contemplate on a scale of 0 to 10 how resilient you are.

Take a quick moment and assess yourself using a scale from 0=10.

0 – I crumble, grumble and despise change

5 – it depends. I may balk or grumble but I can usually recover from change.

10 - I welcome change and embrace all changes with a positive outlook.

I'd love to say I'm a 10 all the time. Sometimes I can be a 10. It all depends on the type of change and how many other changes have occurred in my life at the time. Most of the time I'm a 7-8 and I tend to bounce back quickly.

How resilient are you when change happens?

Take a moment to compare and contrast when you've

bounced back and when you've fallen flat for a bit. How are those two scenarios different? How are they alike? Capture what the main difference was.

In the client examples and coaching vignettes below, see how change and resiliency can present itself. Read on to see how resiliency skills can transform a life and then bleed into transforming others.

A client we'll call Mary starts coaching with the desire to change jobs and get out of the low paying, high stress job she's in. After coaching her it becomes apparent in a few sessions that the low paying, high stress job is a symptom of something deeper. I begin to learn more about her personal life including the person she's chosen to partner with. I learned that Mary is VERY resilient and has survived all kinds of tragedies in her life. The job stress and wanting more money are due to the fact she's now barely making a living wage. She knows how she got to this place, becoming a widow with six kids, bad investments, startup business failure, legal disputes over the kids' trust and overwhelming financial home repairs due to flooding. Despite all of these tragedies, she's ready to move forward and become more like she had been in the past. She was and is an intelligent, college degreed, hard working woman who was on a successful career-high technology engineering path. However, now Mary is stuck and can't seem to find the time to search for a new job in high tech much less take time to research a new job. She's too exhausted at the end of each day. Her work as a day care assistant director seemed like a good idea to help pay bills and be with the kids before she was widowed. She shares that her new partner doesn't work nor does she help around the house at all. She alludes to the fact her partner has fallen out of recovery. Mary's frustrated with the current situation, wants to change but feels stuck. Mary has a heart of gold and gives to everyone-her work, her children, her grandchildren, her partner and her friends.

What kind of resiliency characteristics does Mary exhibit?

She's aware of the changes and knows they've affected her. She's hopeful and knows she can overcome her financial set-backs. She knows that life changes are temporary and she can change her circumstances. She is skilled, educated and knows she has value and is a great contributor to whatever job/career she pursues. She has a strong faith community that has kept her afloat both financially and spiritually and has helped provide for her and her family.

What resiliency characteristics are weaker for Mary?

The first thing we worked on in our coaching sessions was what taking good care of Mary looked like including the two components of self-care and self-compassion. How could Mary stand up for herself and say no in order to take care of herself and promote her dreams. The number one goal that we worked on was boundaries which made a life altering difference. When to say yes and when to say no. We started with healthy boundaries at work by putting up a "Please Do Not Disturb" sign so she would have some quiet, productive work time. Then we moved to healthy boundaries with her one older adult child. The last boundary we explored was how to stop being taken advantage of by her abusive partner. She eventually kicked her out after trying to get her help. She leaned into setting healthy boundaries for all aspects of her life work and her relationships. She's doing amazing now. She has a job that pays well and her boss and staff adore her hard work. She has a new partner that treats her well and cares for her and her children. Mary's adult kid is back in her life and they have a healthier relationship. Resiliency skills can transform a life and others lives too. Did you catch that?

What resonates with you in Mary's story of resiliency?

Now let's look at a client we'll call Bob. Bob is a mid-late career change client. He shows up angry and depressed about being laid off. He feels like a failure; his self-esteem is shot and he has high pressure from home to get a job and keep the family living their accustomed lifestyle. His words to me are, "I need you to help me get unstuck so I can find a job."

I learned that Bob is a smart, talented software engineer with several years of experience in both startup companies and more established tech companies from California to Texas. He is angry about getting laid off and complains they lost the best programmer they ever had. He's depressed they haven't called back to rehire him. Bob beams when he talks about his work and projects he's worked on. He loves his young family and wants to spend more time with them but needs to work as he is the sole breadwinner.

I share my awareness of "angry Bob" and "beaming Bob" with him. He's struck and tearfully gets very quiet. We sit in the silence. Bob whispers, "I just really want to be home with the family and not working all the time. The stress is killing me. I have to take blood pressure medicine at age 32 but I HAVE to get a job and take care of the family."

What resiliency characteristics does Bob exhibit?

Bob wants to make a change and is hopeful that coaching will get him unstuck. He's aware of the stuckness and he's willing to get support. That's the first step in overcoming a challenge. Bob has a solid resume, LinkedIn profile and is networking within his old group of tech buddies. Networking and reaching out are resiliency skills. Bob also has put in the work to update his resume and LinkedIn profile in order to facilitate getting a job. Being prepared for seeking a new job with a resume and updated social media profiles are also resiliency characteristics. He's proactive and taking positive steps to meet the job-seeking challenge. Bob also is willing to acknowledge the reality of what he wants. It's not a job he really wants. He wants to be with his family and not in a high stress job. He is very confident of his skills and talents. He embodies the hot shot coder as he talks about his work and himself. A positive view of his skills and talents are resiliency characteristics.

Over the coaching relationship, the tearful family awareness keeps popping up. We'll be coaching doing great work and boom – we run up against the fact he doesn't really want another soul sucking tech job. He wants to work from home and have the ability to spend time with his family. He's told me this more than once. As quickly as he states that, he dismisses the thought as being a dreamer and unrealistic. He HAS to take care of his family and get another job. When we examine this belief , he gets quiet. He then tears up and gets angry. "Stop poking me, I'm NOT going to do anything stupid like start his own consulting business or ask to work from home. I mean I'm interviewing. I hired you to help me get a job."

What resiliency characteristics are weaker for Bob?

Bob lacks a positive view of his future and sees only one solution. He is begrudgingly getting another tech job to pay the bills and keep his family happy. He's unwilling to dive into what makes him angry and sad about having to get a tech job. He will acknowledge the job isn't what he really wants but that he's unwilling to explore the possibilities. "Nope, I won't go there", he repeats. When he retires then he can then indulge himself. In working with him, I also discovered that self-care isn't a priority he's willing to commit to. I also notice that he's unwilling to set healthy boundaries around work. It is his life and he's comfortable with this being his addiction and it's what makes him a success.

What other resiliency characteristics did you notice with Mary and Bob? What resiliency characteristics do you see in your clients?

At the conclusion of the coaching relationship Mary realized she was worthy of self care and she didn't need to be a people pleaser. She found boundary setting to be critical for her success. Bob found another job in high tech that has some flexibility and is able to spend more time with his family. He continues to pop in and out of coaching and still refuses to "go there" when we get to self-care and doing what he really wants. As a coach, it's important to know you cannot push your clients into more self-awareness and resiliency **than they are ready for at that time.**

Let's take a look at resiliency characteristics in a list format. You can use this list to get curious about your own resiliency.

Resiliency Characteristics Short List

1. Viewing change as an opportunity.

2. Thinking of life changes as temporary.

3. Believing that no crisis is too great.

4. Having a positive view of the future.

5. Having confidence in your skills and talents.

6. Committing to self, family or spiritual beliefs

7. Networking - make and keep connections with groups (social, religious, family, volunteer, professional ICF...)

8. Forming healthy boundaries in all relationships (professional, family, friends)

9. Maintaining healthy boundaries for self (stand up and be seen and heard, do not be taken advantage of and be comfortable saying "no")

10. Showing empathy and compassion

11. Demonstrating compassion for self

12. Mitigating strategies for obstacles

13. Creating new options when life changes

14. Checking in with your heart passion – what gives you energy or sucks the life out of you

15. Breaking problems down into small chunks

16. Making goals and taking action to complete them

17. Journaling one thing to improve today

What did you notice about the list? About your resiliency? Rate yourself high, medium, low as you reread the list. How would you rate your resiliency overall? Where might you want to build more resiliency skills?

Building more resiliency

1. Understanding your beliefs about change impact resiliency.

Your beliefs about change impact your resiliency. This statement is derived from Albert Ellis's Rational Emotive Behavior – ABCD where the letters stand for looking at change from the perspective of the Activating Event, Beliefs about the event, Consequences of the change, and lastly Dispelling any negative thoughts and beliefs.

Here's a scenario to demonstrate how beliefs about a change can shape us.

You have to download a new software program as an upgrade to your work portal. It's going to fix "everything" and be "great." When you hear this – do you jump for joy and think, "Oh good. Those bugs will be fixed and I can't wait to download or do you "roll your eyes and think, here we go again. This will definitely crash my system?"

Imagine if you had a jump-for-joy belief even if it does crash your system. What if you had a positive thought about the upgrade? You'd be more likely to bounce back **regarding the change due to positive beliefs about the upgrade. If you're procrastinating and avoi**ding the upgrade and worried it will crash your system, you're not working through the change nor exhibiting resiliency.

What negative beliefs might you be holding onto that may not be helping you in times of change?

What is your typical response to change? Embracing it, making the changes, seeking transformation?

2. Develop positive view of change

Now that we know our beliefs about change impact our resiliency, we can use that knowledge to build the next skill. The next skill is having the capacity to view change in a positive light. If we are able to look at the good learning and/or opportunity in a change, we're building a resilient mindset.

How do we embrace this when the change is a challenge or awful in our perception? Let's think back to the start of the pandemic. I imagine your first reaction wasn't, "Oh, goodies! Let's see the good." However, as time went by the world began to slow down; we began to enjoy more time at the slower pace at home. We became grateful for the pause. We were building resiliency while being quarantined.

3. Realize this change isn't forever – it's a season of life

When changes occur, we can feel like the immediate freak out will last forever. The event and change may **feel like it will last forever. Many changes will not sustain over time. It's important to note that our feelings about the event are not permanent either.. They will not last forever. The intensity of our** feelings of fear, pain or joy are temporary. Feelings change. Looking to the future is a resiliency trait. Knowing and seeking the light at the end of the tunnel can build resiliency. Resilient people know that when changes occur it's only for a season of life. What season of life are you in? What might the light at the end of the tunnel be?

4. Set professional and personal boundaries

Having healthy boundaries is a key characteristic for resilient people. Saying yes to what you want to and no to what you don't want is the simple definition I use. If you find you cannot say no and have said yes to too many things, it may be time to take inventory of your boundaries. Knowing and keeping your boundaries in all areas of your life are vital to bouncing back from changes. Evaluating your boundaries at home, work and with family is a great place to start. Reviewing and revitalizing healthy boundaries are a sign of resiliency.

5. Connection – Who is in your network of life?

Your circle of people in your life and having a diverse network are resiliency characteristics. When change happens, you can utilize your network for resources, accountability and support. Think of all the networks in your life and the people involved. Consider family and other groups such as religious, professional, volunteer, hobby, social, work and recreation. This is a great place to start. Make a thorough list. Think about the people in each group and make a list of those people who you know you can ask for support and help.

6. Planning, goal setting and taking action

Resilient people have the capacity to plan, set goals and then work towards those goals. I coach many people with time management issues that have beautiful planners with color coded "do's" that have difficulty getting things accomplished. The key is to set SMART goals as a living process. Then after setting the goals the second key is taking action towards those goals.

Another hint for taking action to move forward is breaking down your goals into smaller doable steps. Finally, a key to continue reaching your goals is to celebrate the mini goals along the way. If celebrating feels strange, then take time to acknowledge your hard work. I realize this sounds easy and may be easier said than done for many people. In coaching we support our clients in the goal setting and help them be accountable in achieving their goals.

You now have six different ways to build your own resiliency and that of your clients. You now are aware that your beliefs about change impact resiliency; a positive view of change builds resiliency; feelings about the change aren't forever; boundaries are important; a diverse network is key; and planning and taking action sets us up for success.

How else might you build your resiliency? What goals will you set? Who can help hold you accountable? How will you acknowledge or celebrate your goals?

Powerful Coaching Questions for Resiliency

For those of you who are not coaches you can ask yourself these questions to assess and build your resiliency. If you are a coach you can incorporate these into your practice to support your client's growth and awareness.

- How do you know it's time to bounce back?

- What's the story you're telling yourself about this situation?

- What is the major obstacle to moving forward?

- What challenges have you experienced?

- Describe in vivid detail your proudest moment.

- How are you personalizing the event?

- How is this your fault? How often do you say I'm sorry?

- How pervasive is this event? What's the impact on you?

    - What are you grateful for?

    - How permanent is the event? How long might this last?

    - What if this were a season of life?

    - What do you have control over?

    - What boundary do you want/need to set?

- What have you survived before?

- What resources can you rely upon (people, places, things?)

- How can you nurture yourself? (self-care)

My hope is that you've learned something about resiliency. Maybe you've learned about your resiliency. Maybe you have some new tools to use with coaching. Keep growing your resiliency.

Resiliency Reflections:

- What have you learned by reading this?

- What has changed now that you know the definition of resiliency and have explored the characteristics?

- How might you utilize this knowledge to help yourself and others?

- How might you answer the provocative, powerful questions to explore resiliency?

- What is one next step you're willing to take toward building your own resiliency?

May you bounce back more easily from change.

Peace & Blessings, Teresa Bitner

Bio

Teresa partners with those who've been knocked down by life and want to bounce back to live a more bold life. She's a coach, speaker, and author specializing in resiliency, change, and loss. Change happens in life and work. Building resiliency and learning steps for surviving and thriving amidst constant change sets apart those who live boldly.

Teresa is about giving back and service. She volunteers with International Coaching Federation (ICF) Austin is a former Board Member – Community Outreach Director organizing pro bono coaching to local nonprofits. She is on the coaching bench for Women for Change Coaching Community (W4C3) - providing pro-bono coaching to women in poverty. She also is a Stand Beside Them Coach – providing pro-bono coaching for veterans and their spouses. InviteChange coach for non-profit leaders. You can learn more, connect, find her blog and books at www.boldfulfilledlifecoach.com.

THE ART AND IMPACT OF QUESTIONS

By Diane Dean, MA, MCC

What is our purpose as coaches to ask questions? One reason is to refrain from "telling", as a consultant might give advice. In any context, we humans ask questions to understand what the other person means or is trying to express. Often misinterpretation happens even when you are speaking with a person who speaks your own language. We often think maybe we didn't pay attention as well as we should have or that the other person is "unclear". Misunderstandings abound in many situations, even between friends, business partners and spouses.

What the developers of Neuro Linguistic Programming observed and codified starts with the differences between CONTENT we speak of and PROCESS of how we get our thoughts into language. Communication has these two specific components that impact how questions work. One component is the CONTENT. The other component is the PROCESS. If you manage your process in a way to keep the conversation going, addressing the kind of information you desire, you can often sort out the content and reach greater understanding of the other's point of view.

One couple of business partners, before learning more about the process, would get stuck in content. Very stuck. They would abandon a discussion, not very productive, because they didn't realize how to ask each other and themselves useful questions to keep exploring their issue to a conclusion. The mismatches were "in their brains" so discussion was stuck on content. We will learn Lynn and Bob's solution later in this article.

The "misunderstanding" happening in our brains has been discussed at length by neuroscience for a few years. According to David Eagleman, neuroscientist and author of *The Brain: The Story of You*, "the brain has no access to the world outside. ...your brain has never directly experienced the external world and it never will." He goes as far to say that "reality is a construction of your brain, taking place only in your head" - your experience of reality or your own Mental Model.

In addition, "Your brain predicts what the scene should look like and feel like, then it generates a hallucination that you experience in the world around you. ...This hallucinated reconstruction of reality is sometimes referred to as the brain's "model of the world." (June, 2020 Scientific American) This concept continues to be affirmed through research and neuroscience.

Decades ago, researchers began exploring the idea of Mental Models or Models of the World as I learned about it in my NLP Training. Wikipedia sums up a mental model as an explanation of someone's thought process; its representation of how another person is thinking. Though mental models have been discussed, studied and written about for decades, neuroscience currently supports the idea that "it's all in our heads"! If you are a "brain nerd" like I am, I suggest reading David Eagleman's work.

Eagleman explains that mental models help us understand the other person's thought process about their view of the world. The bottom line is that we all need good questions to get the information we need to understand another person's mental representation. The image of the world around us, which we carry in our head, is just a model.

As coaches, what does this mean to our understanding of others, or not? It means we need to ask questions to understand our clients in a way that we can "Meet them where they are!"

The Art and Impact of Questions offers coaches tools to "peel back the onion" on another person's model of the world--getting closer to understanding how your client is thinking and experiencing their reality. Questions are approached as a system of tools that help you, the coach, understand the client's approach to reasoning, decision-making and perceptions. Questions can transform thinking, action and results on the whole ,while expanding the clarity of understanding of your thinking and your client's. After using these tools for over 30 years, I'm still thrilled when a client says, "Oh, that's a really good question!"

When a client is stuck (or we are), we need to change our questions. At times we may get into a routine of the same old questions and what do we get? The same old responses! New questions, different questioning patterns, can shift perspectives for the client and ourselves.

I operate on the belief that clients have all the needed resources within themselves to make their desired changes. It is the coach's job to help the client uncover or discover those within themselves. Strategic questions are the tools we need.

In this section, we'll explore five key questioning patterns that will empower your ability to understand your clients' interpretations of the world they live in....in their mental models. Communication has a structure and we have learned our version of it or parts of it. We get into habits some of which work and some do not.

Are you talking about what you WANT or what you DON'T WANT?

I was asked to speak with the Austin Women in Technology (AWT) at their monthly mentoring session. Some of the questions they wanted answered were:

1. How to effectively communicate in a primarily male field

2. How to create an impact and influence other

3. How to resolve conflict

The questions we will explore are tools to answer "how".

It is a gross generalization to say "males communicate differently than females" as a whole gender. This had been many AWT women's experience in the technology field or rather how they have interpreted how they hear men. What is fairly consistent in my experience, working at a technology company myself for 10+ years, is that engineers are problem solvers. They get into the field being motivated by "fixing" situations that aren't working, especially mechanical or technical kinds of issues.

On the other hand, there are many people of any gender, who look to options, solutions or creative alternatives. My colleagues and I teach communication to allow people to work with the various patterns people use. Let's look at two sets of questions. These two sets of questions exemplify either "fixers" or "creators". As you consider the next example, notice which set resonates with your patterns.

We will explore the two business partners who have worked together for over six years and are still getting stuck trying to move forward in their business planning at times. We introduced them earlier. They would get into a push/pull discussion. I will share the questions they began to utilize to successfully get on with their planning.

For example, Bob would follow this pattern essentially:

- What's the problem?
- Why do we have it?
- Who and what is limiting us or preventing getting what we want?

- Whose fault is it?

These aren't his identical questions but the general process followed these lines.

Lynn, on the other hand, went down a different path with her search for answers:

- What is our desired outcome? What do we want?

- How will we know when we attain it? Get there?

- What possibilities might exist based on our current situation?

- What have we learned from this situation so far?

What are the differences between these two sets of questions? In one model, the motivation and questions search out the problem to be solved or fixed. This is called the PROBLEM or BLAME Frame in the communication workshop we taught. The second set of questions is called the OUTCOME or AIM Frame. We are aiming at what we do want, not what we don't want! Motivation is coming from creating answers and solutions.

What changed? Two sets of questions came out (not the exact words, but the intent--solve a problem or create a solution.) This may seem like the same and it's not in terms of content OR process of communication.

The following is a quote from Lynn based on what these partners learned about motivation guiding their thinking from attending a Syntax workshop.

"My co-founder and I took the training together and were pleasantly surprised to discover new things about each other and about our collaboration as a team. In one of the exercises, we discovered that he was motivated by problems and I am motivated by solutions. This made a big lightbulb go off for us around why we may shy away from various conversations. It also has helped us move forward by being sure that I focus on roles that are solution oriented and he focuses on roles that are problem oriented. With that alignment we are much more productive and effective as a leadership team. It has also helped us as we lead our teams, to understand better how our team members are motivated."

One book I read called the different motivators "Judger questions and Learner questions". No matter what the questions are called, the different patterns change outcomes and sometimes stop the disagreeing conversations! And they can keep the productive conversations open!

Verify

Much is written about Active Listening and it's a good tool for some things. This is a definition I found on Google that sums it up very well:

"Active listening refers to a pattern of listening that keeps you engaged with your conversation partner in a positive way. It is the process of listening attentively while someone else speaks, paraphrasing and reflecting back what is said and withholding judgment and advice.

The benefit is mainly that the conversation partner feels, well, listened to. Whether he or she is understood is another thing altogether."

I would agree with this definition. Active Listening is usually most effective in creating and keeping rapport, a large aspect of connecting with your client. And Active Listening doesn't always include a component of "questioning to understand".

There is a rather simple process that will help you understand your client's model of the world better, fairly quickly.

While working with "hallucinations" or models of the world, we hear from *our* brains, and subsequently "interpret" what the client means. This is often not a match. Coaches need to take the time to check in with the client to more fully understand what the other person means. This "check in" is called Verifying or Verification. "What skilled communicators do is to separate raw data--the information collected by the senses--from how it is interpreted." (Lucy Freedman, *Smart Work* P80.)

Some ways to verify for understanding are:

Do you mean...?

So, what you are telling me is...?

What I understand you to say is...is that what you mean?

Let me playback what I think we've determined so far...Do I have it?

Your question will share your interpretation of what you heard. This is very helpful to "get on the same page." Verifying is a good way to review what has been discussed and be sure you are aligned. The following is an example of understanding through verifying and impacting perspective as well.

Mack, a Comptroller, was sent to coaching because his communication style was making for an uncooperative work environment, the President said. In the first two sessions, Mack was understandably defensive as he felt criticized about his management style. He had a belief that his employees, one in particular, didn't like him and just resisted to "have his own way." I begin probing a bit with verifying what I understood him to say or mean. This process not only verifies, it gives the client a "peek" at his/her impact with certain statements.

My verification to the statement above was, "Mack, do you mean this employee isn't doing his job properly because he doesn't want to be told what to do?" The phrasing was intentional--"told what to do"--very different from "doing his job" or "have his own way." At least, how the question landed gave Mack a moment of pause and time to think. I also asked Mack if he ever asked this particular person some questions to understand his thinking or get his opinions, a process I was modeling with Mack. He rarely did, he said.

To make a long, but successful story short, Mack began to study communication reading *Smart Work: The Syntax Guide to Influence.* This is a book I often refer to when communication appears to be the issue. As he applied what he learned from the book, he studied his behavior very diligently. I've never seen a leader who so quickly began to work so hard. As he began to be successful with the "problem employee", a light bulb went off. Mack said, "I realized, when I was in law school, they said they would change the way we think and they did!" He was still speaking to employees as if he were a prosecutor!! (He practiced law for 15 years.)

Mack recognized people didn't want to work for him because he questioned people in an aggressive way and found what was not working, criticizing. After studying and being in coaching for about six months, he attended my workshop on communication and influence. He changed his behavior to the degree his President wrote me a letter praising Mack. Mack reported "All my relationships, even with my wife, have improved." So good to hear people get benefits they desire.

Verify frequently, <u>rephrase</u> what you heard, and you will reduce the effect of your mental model taking over the meaning and you will be more likely to align with your client's meaning.

Why not ask Why?

Toyota car company started a process long ago called The Five Why Method. "The 5 Whys technique is a simple and effective tool for solving problems. Its primary goal is to find the exact reason that causes a given problem by asking a sequence of "Why" questions. The 5 Whys method helps your team focus on finding the root cause of any problem." Critical in this definition that makes it successful in the world of mechanical engineering and other forms of technology is "finding the root cause".

In my experience, asking WHY often focuses on an undesired pattern of information and some responses I don't want. Consider how it feels when you are asked WHY, like "Why would you do THAT?" "Why is this happening?" "Why didn't you…" We often create excuses, justifications and rationalizations that don't get us anywhere toward our outcomes and goals.

What often happens when a person answers WHY is that we get **justification, generalization, deletion or distortion** which are naturally occurring linguistic patterns. We all have these patterns. Sometimes we might get wisdom from why. If you want and need specific information you need different strategic questions that get to it. I avoid WHY from my questioning as it doesn't help me gather useful, more specific information. To do this, I use WHO, WHAT, HOW, WHEN, WHERE vs why.

Sometimes people do bring up the Toyota 5 Why process. The Toyota Why process has a different desired outcome which is to discover the root cause. The team members are all focused on the same outcome--solving a problem that they all agree is a problem. As a coach, I don't believe that's what I am looking for.

My goal is to help the other person discover their own resources for tackling what they interpret as problems or limits.

SUMMARY

- Meet the person "where they are"—learn their Mental Model

- AIM FRAME vs BLAME FRAME—manage the questions to align and get to what you DO want vs what you don't want

- Remember to verify what is being said—different Models of the World

- Use WHAT, HOW, WHICH, WHEN, AND WHERE vs WHY

My suggestion is to pick a section and practice the questioning distinctions one at a time. You probably use these questions already and you can be more strategic regarding when you employ certain questioning patterns. Best wishes on using these skills to continue being a good coach with influence!

Resources:

Coaching with NLP, Joseph O'Connor and Andrea Lages

Change Your Questions, Change Your Life, Marilee G. Adams, Ph.D.

The Brain: The Story of You, David Eagleman

Smart Work: The Syntax Guide to Influence, edition 2; Lucy Freedman and Lisa Marshall

Bio

Expertise in how people learn and communicate enables Diane to cut short the time it takes people to learn new ways to approach situations that may be delaying their personal or organization development. An Executive Coach since 1988 and Master Certified Coach with the International Coach Federation since 2000, Diane's skills and experience help guide career focus and your decision process.

Areas of Expertise

Diane's experience includes executive and management coaching, career management, communication, leadership development, presentation skills and meeting facilitation. Leadership development includes the use of 360° Feedback Surveys with coaching and action planning.

Certifications include Certified Trainer of NLP, Senior Consultant for Syntax for Change, Certified in Global Team Coaching Gateway Program. For 10+ years, Diane led Learning & Development for Tokyo Electron, US Holdings.

The Learner's Edge Coaching and Consulting, www.thelearnersedege.com 512-293-3815

COACHING THE LEGENDARY LIFE

How a Boy's Adventure Influenced My Coaching

By Michelle Hefner, ACC

"Metaphor and myth are the means by which we inform and instruct ourselves."--Joseph Campbell

A few years ago, a client of mine asked if I would coach her, her husband, Dave, and their 11 year old son, Luke, in an equine assisted coaching session. She and I had met at a meditation retreat months before. She became intrigued by the idea of working with the horses after I described them as 1000 lb. biofeedback machines, responding at all times to your energetic state. After having several powerful sessions with my horses, Sara thought her son would benefit from working with them . She wanted to work with him on confidence, communication and trust before he headed off to his first year of middle school.

Although I had spent 12 years as a middle school and high school teacher, that career was in the distant past. The prospect felt daunting within the typical hour and a half timeframe of most equine sessions. Fortunately, I knew beyond a shadow of a doubt that my horse, Snickers, would cover the confidence part of the equation. Horses simply will not follow anyone until the person embodies confidence. My job would be to facilitate communication and build trust between the boy, his parents, the horse and me as the coach. Holding space for the cultivation of trust, the heart of our work as coaches, would require some consideration, though, since I had never met this young man and I had never coached a child.

Pondering how I would create a connection with Luke, an idea came to me. I asked his mother what his favorite movie was. Her answer was, unequivocally, *The Avengers*. As I watched the movie, I was struck by what was playing out on the screen. I knew what to do. Luke would be the mythological superhero in a metaphorical adventure. Snickers would be his companion, his mom and dad would fill the roles of mentor and ally. Together, this team would accompany Luke as characters in their own unforgettable story of leadership, communication, adventure and trust.

What had struck me was the fact that the movie followed the same storyline as described by Joseph Campbell, professor of comparative mythology, in his 1949 book, The Hero with a Thousand Faces. In it, he brought awareness to a common dramatic arc shared by stories the world over--a hero called to an adventure who first refuses the call. He must wrestle with inner and/or outer demons as he meets mentors and allies along the way. In the end, the hero experiences a profound inner transformation and returns, victorious. Dr. Campbell called this template the "Hero's Journey".

As coaches we believe in our clients' success until they believe it for themselves. I was so certain of Luke's triumph as the hero that I bought a wax seal set and some parchment paper. I made a rolled scroll, sealing it with an ornate wax stamp. It was an official proclamation of Luke's new hero status to be presented to him in a final ceremony at the end of our session.

The following is the story of Luke's experiences in his own hero's journey, his personal, fantastical adventure. It is followed by how you might use the template in your coaching.

Stage 1--The Ordinary World

"Mythology is to relate found truth to the living of life."--Joseph Campbell

The "Hero's Journey" begins by exploring his present, everyday life, his safe space, his inherent nature and his outlook on life. It is here that we learn crucial details about him, his core beliefs, capabilities, values and self view. We discover how he perceives his position in society and how he relates to those around him.

Before giving Luke the map to the maze I had made in my horse arena, I asked him his feelings around entering middle school. Without making eye contact, the boy hesitantly admitted he was scared about making new friends and having to go to a new school. "What if this were simply a new adventure in your life?" I asked. He shuffled his feet, quietly staring at the ground.

When I told him I had watched *The Avengers*, his eyes lit up, his energy shifted in a flash and he animatedly shared his favorite parts of the movie. I asked him if today he would be the superhero in an adventure. Snickers could be his guide and companion along the way. He fidgeted with the lead line connected to the horse's halter and said, "I don't know anything about horses." "That's OK. Snickers' job is to teach you how to be a confident leader and your parents are also here to help you. It will be up to you to tell them, though, how they can be of help. Oh, and they can only help you for the first half of the maze." Luke looked doubtfully around at the cones, the barrels and the poles spread out around the arena. Snickers opened his mouth in a giant yawn, his tongue flapping out to one side and his eyes rolling back in his head. This horse has a gift for lightening any situation.

Stage 2--The Call to Adventure.

"The hero's journey always begins with the call. One way or another, a guide must come to say, 'Look, you're in Sleepy Land. Wake. Come on a trip. There is a whole aspect of your consciousness, your being, that's not been touched. So you're at home here? Well there's not enough of you there.' And so it starts."--Joseph Cambell

The hero's adventure begins when he receives a call to action. This call rattles the comfort of his ordinary world and presents a challenge of some sort. From this point, nothing will remain the same as before. He experiences a compulsion from within and without, pushing him to act. The call could be for a life change or an offer of a new opportunity. Whatever it is, it requires venturing into the unknown and taking a risk.

For Luke, the unknown was going into a new grade level, a new school and needing to make new friends. I asked Luke to assign a title to his present life. He thought for a moment and said, "Baseball and Fun". "And if we were to give a title to the next chapter, what might it be?" I continued. His face scrunched into a worrying frown and he said, simply, "Scared".

Stage 3--Refusal of the Call.

"The cave you fear to enter holds the treasure you seek."--Joseph Campbell

In myths and legends, trepidation often causes the hero to initially refuse the call to adventure. He may have second thoughts or personal doubts that cause him to vacillate. The problem might feel overwhelming and the desire to stay home strong but, like Luke, the hero really does not have a choice.

In the round arena, no sooner had Luke started off on his journey than Snickers stopped in his tracks in response to the boy's lack of confidence. Luke's face was downcast. He looked ready to give up. His dad stepped in to offer advice and to help Luke overcome any fears he had with the horse. He told Luke to look to his future with an air of certainty and to imagine what a leader might look like. The subtle shift in Luke's posture and the slight look of determination that came across his face did not go unnoticed by the small, Arabian horse. When Luke started again, Snickers followed. Soon, the pair approached the first obstacle--a small jump they needed to step over. Snickers thought it would be easier to go around the pole rather than over it. Luke circled several times with the horse and each time Snickers chose to walk around the obstacle. Luke looked to his mom and said, "He won't go over it." Luke again seemed on the verge of giving up.

I asked him, "What do you usually do when you've tried something two or three times and it doesn't go as planned?" "Sometimes I just think I can't do it and I try not to care anymore," he said. I asked him to make "I can't do it" into a villainous character in his adventure. Luke named his villain Dr. Don't and assigned him the supervillain power of making people stop trying. Next, Luke explored how he could battle Dr. Don't. His mother suggested that the villain's weakness could be people's persistence. Then, she said, "What do you need from me? How can I help?" Luke thought for a minute and then directed her to be a "wall" to block the side where Snickers had repeatedly gone around the pole. Now Snickers had no choice but to walk over the obstacle with Luke. Persistence became Luke's key weapon in battling Dr. Don't and he found that, like with any new skill, it required practice.

Stage 4--Meeting the Mentor

"When the hero is ready, the mentor appears."--Will Craig

At this point, the hero needs additional guidance. He looks for a mentor amongst his companions who can give him support on his journey. His mentor might give him an object of great importance, wise advice, needed insight, training or self confidence. The mentor's gift dissolves the hero's doubts and fears and gives him courage to continue on his quest.

When it was time for Luke to choose a mentor, I explained that the role of the mentor is to show us the way, believe in us more than we do and help us find the courage, strength and wisdom we didn't know we had. He said, "Oh, like Nick Fury!" "Yes!," I replied, "from SHIELD". (The intelligence agency in the movie). Luke chose his father without hesitation, saying, "He already told me how to be a leader and it worked!" I then had Dave choose a gift from an array of objects I had placed on a table that could serve as a symbol for Luke. Dave chose a horseshoe and said it was imbued with the speed of a horse and the strength of iron. Luke hung it on his belt and said it could represent "courage". Dave promised to continue supporting Luke and giving him advice on his journey.

Stage 5--Crossing the Threshold

"It has always been the prime function of mythology and rite to supply the symbols that carry the human spirit forward, in counteraction to those that tend to hold it back."--Joseph Campbell

The hero is now ready to truly begin his quest, fully committing to the adventure. He crosses the threshold between the world he has known and the new, unknown world. This requires a leap of faith on his part and he must now learn to navigate the sea of vulnerability to support his courage. In preparation, he has learned from those around him and tapped into his creative inner resources. It is time for him to fully engage his wisdom, intuition and inherent gifts.

By the quarter mark in the arena, Luke had become a more confident leader as evidenced by Snickers following him wherever he set his sights. As he crossed the threshold (a chalk line between 2 barrels), the obstacles became a little more challenging. I asked him what he wanted his catchphrase to be. He grabbed his horseshoe off of his belt and shouted, "Fear Nothing!" The shy, quiet boy I had met just 20 minutes prior had transformed before my eyes. His tone of voice and facial expressions had all expanded in tandem with his posture. There was even a hint of mischief previously lacking.

Stage 6--Tests, Allies, Enemies

"... the tests, the allies, and the enemies all prepare us to face and overcome the great challenge that awaits us, the challenge to be and to do more than the ordinary, the challenge to transform ourselves and the world."--Joseph Campbell

Now, out of his comfort zone, the hero is confronted with an ever more difficult series of challenges that test him in a variety of ways. Physical hurdles, inner doubts and other people threaten to impede his progress. He will meet foes and will have to discern between those who will help him and those who wish for his failure, those he can trust and those he cannot. He meets allies who will help him prepare for the greater ordeals yet to come. His skills and powers are tested and he will need to muster his resources, knowledge, intuition and courage to succeed.

Naming his allies, the first on Luke's list was Sara, his mom. Following her were his 2 best friends on his baseball team and then Snickers. I asked how his mom and Snickers might help him as he navigated the more complicated obstacles ahead. He said that Sara was always there for him, believing in him and supporting him. She promised to share suggestions with him and help in any way she could think of. Snickers, for his part, snorted, blinked his big, brown eyes and head butted Luke in the lower back, propelling the boy forward. Luke laughed and said Snickers would keep him on track and not let him give up.

As Luke and Snickers continued their journey, he found more and more that he needed the help of his parents to navigate the difficult obstacles. When they reached some low hanging, colorful pool noodles, Snickers stopped in his tracks while Luke went through them alone. The boy tried again, pulling on the lead line with all of his might. The stocky horse barely noticed, still refusing to budge. Sara suggested the horse might be afraid of the noodles. A frustrated Luke replied, "But he saw me go under them first. He's been following me this far." His dad added, "Maybe he doesn't trust that it's safe." "How can I make him go?" Luke asked. I asked Luke if, at some point, he might have lost connection with Snickers. He said, "Well, he was walking with me and then he stopped and I kept going. Maybe that was it." I said, "It's one thing to be a confident leader but what else do you need for trust?"

The family huddled together and decided what was needed to maintain trust was connection, honest communication, support and reliability. They made a plan. They surrounded the horse and all placed a hand on him. Encouraging him to move forward with them as a group, they praised him for each step he took. Finally on the other side of the noodles, Snickers did a full body shake, moving the energy of the experience through himself and releasing it. Dave and Luke hi-fived while Sara cheered.

Stage 7--Approach to the Inmost Cave

"It is going down into the abyss that we recover the treasures of life. Where you stumble, there lies your treasure."--Joseph Campbell

In myths and legends, the inmost cave can be an actual location wherein lies a serious danger or an inner conflict the hero has yet to address. Here, the hero might again face some of the same doubts and fears he faced when first called to adventure. This is a moment for him to reflect on his journey, the road ahead and muster the courage to continue.

At the halfway point of the maze, Luke reviewed his adventure thus far. He described how, in the beginning, he was nervous, not knowing anything about horses. There had been several times where he wanted to give up. Each time he doubted himself, Snickers refused to follow. He had to turn to his parents for help, telling them what he needed so they would know what to do. He listed the lessons he had learned along the way. He said his mom had taught him about persistence and his dad and Snickers taught him about confidence and trust. This knowledge made him stronger. Dr. Don't was no match for him now. His magic horseshoe would help him maintain his courage in the face of anything! From this point on, he and Snickers were on their own. He used all of the knowledge and mastery he gained during the first half of the journey to create a plan.

Stage 8--The Supreme Ordeal

"And where we had thought to slay another we shall slay ourselves. Where we had thought to travel outwards we shall come to the center of our own existence."--Joseph Campbell

The Supreme Ordeal can be a dangerous, physical test, an inner crisis or a monster of some sort that the hero must battle to save the world. The hero must draw upon all of the skills and experiences he has gathered to overcome his most difficult challenge. He experiences a metaphorical transformation that grants him greater power or insight that will help him reach the journey's end. After this point in the story the hero's life will never again be the same. It is time for him to fulfill his destiny.

Luke and Snickers continued through the maze until they reached a wall. This spot would be the scene of his imaginary battle against a demon. I explained to Luke that often, in stories and movies, the demons represent the negative emotions inside us all. These include frustration, anxiety, anger, shame, jealousy, annoyance... I watched as the wheels in his head were turning. "Loki (again from the movie) is always making trouble. He likes to turn people against each other. Maybe he represents jealousy," he said excitedly.

I asked him which demon he wanted to fight. He said he wanted to fight Anger. I had him close his eyes and imagine anger as a physical form. "What does anger look like?" I asked. His brow furrowed, his eyes closed more tightly and he said, "He's really big and made of fire. He's scary. His eyes are glowing red and look really mean!" "Now," I said, "ask Anger what he needs from you." There was a long silence. His face softened. He inhaled deeply and shared in a barely audible voice, "He needs love." I told him to imagine sending all of the love he could muster towards the demon of anger. After a moment, I asked, "What does he look like now?" Luke slowly opened his eyes. The sun caught the hint of tears pooling in his lower lids. "He's no longer made of fire," he responded sweetly.

Stage 9--The Reward

"Opportunities to find deeper powers within ourselves come when life seems most challenging."--Joseph Campbell

After defeating the enemy, surviving death and finally overcoming great personal challenges, the hero is transformed into a new state, emerging from battle as a new person, often with a prize. The reward may come in many forms: an object of great significance or power, a secret, greater knowledge or a profound insight. As he prepares for the road back to his ordinary life, he recognizes he is a changed man. Life as he knew it would never be the same.

After slaying the demon of Anger, Luke said he had a confession to make. He had been in several fights during the previous school year. This evidently came as a surprise to his parents because they only knew of one. It seems on several occasions three different boys had teased him at school, causing him to become angry and lash out. He added that when they made fun of him, he felt like he just turned into the Hulk, like Bruce, the character in the movie, does. He said he was ashamed and didn't want his parents to know. Dave, in his role as mentor, asked him what he had learned from this 'battle' with anger today. Luke said it made him realize that he really just wanted to be liked and he got really angry when he felt like he wasn't liked. He said that those boys were angry, too and they probably needed love. He felt sorry for them. The next time he met a bully, he said, he would see the fiery demon inside them and feel sadness for the kid instead of anger. Snickers licked, chewed and snorted in agreement.

Stage 10--The Return with the Elixir

"The conquest of fear yields the courage of life. That is the cardinal initiation of every heroic adventure--fearlessness and achievement."--Joseph Campbell

The final stage of the hero's journey is a return home to his ordinary world as a changed man. He will have grown as a person, faced dangers and learned many things. He arrives home as a man of two realms, bringing fresh hope to those he left behind and sharing a new perspective for everyone to consider. Even though he returns to the place he started, his transformation means things will never be the same as they were before the adventure.

After Luke completed his 'battle' with anger, he made his way through the rest of the maze with Snickers. Missing was the hesitancy of before, now replaced with an air of confidence and pride. When he arrived back at the place where he and Snickers had started, I gave him the rolled, wax-sealed scroll. He broke the seal, unrolled it to find his Hero certificate. His parents took photos of Luke holding the certificate in one hand, the lead line in the other with Snickers at his side. The horseshoe, hanging on his belt, glinted in the sunlight. His smile told the story.

"You are the hero of your own story.The privilege of a lifetime is being who you are."-Joseph Campbell

Coaching the Hero's Journey started with a desire to connect with this young boy but it became a powerful tool for coaching adults as well. For some clients, we will complete the cycle in one session. For others, this becomes a template that lasts over the course of our engagement. The power of the story meta-phor is that it bypasses the analytical mind and lights up the creative centers of the brain, making it unforgettable. Once a client has created their legendary story, I find they refer back to it often.They begin recognizing the different chapters of their lives and the overarching themes.

Over the past couple of years, Luke's mother has reported on his progress in school and their relationship. He still refers back to that day and has assigned themes to the trials and tribula-tions of middle school. Recently, she said he was busy planning his next "book" as he prepares to begin High School in the Fall. The magical horseshoe his father chose for him hangs above the door to his bedroom. Underneath it is one word. Courage.

Coaching The Hero's Journey

The Ordinary World

Exploring the "Ordinary World" provides an opportunity to examine the culture of our client's daily life. The client as hero analyzes her current situation, her aspirations, how she experi-ences the world around her and what has led her to this moment in time. She may also assign themes to the various seasons of her life.

- What does the hero of the story care about more than life itself?

- How has the hero been in service to mankind?

- What are the core beliefs that drive our hero?

- What is the hero's ultimate goal?

- To further develop the character of the hero in this story, she considers what else should be added pertaining to the hero's true nature, strengths and outlook on life.

The Call to Adventure

Often, people seek coaching because their lives are shifting in ways that demand some sort of change or that offer a glimpse of new opportunity. It may not be dramatic but any change can be uncomfortable or exhilarating when it requires a move into the unknown. Whatever the shift, it disrupts their ordinary world in some way and presents a challenge that must be undertaken. The following questions will help the client begin the narrative of their life.

- What is the hero in their story being called to do?

- Who else in the hero's life will be impacted?

- What resources and skills does their character currently have that will assist them?

- What creative title can the client give the story that describes it up to this point?

- What might the title of the next chapter be?

Refusal of the Call

This part of the arc provides an opportunity to delve into all of the invented stories that have been useful for the client/hero in making sense of her world. Limiting beliefs are the major culprit that generates resistance to the unknown. Turning doubts and limiting beliefs into characters in the story can help the client begin to manage her mindset and to realize that thoughts are not necessarily reality. By naming these beliefs and making them characters in her story, she can begin to distance herself from the grip of the associated thoughts and emotions.

- If you were to create characters for the story, based on these limiting beliefs, what would they look like? What would their names be? What personality quirks might they have?

- From where might these thoughts have originated?

- How have they limited the hero's experiences in the past?

Meeting the Mentor

It is empowering for the client to reflect upon her resources at hand and consider all of her extended support systems.

- How might her hero draw on that support to aid her?

- Which qualities would she like in a mentor?

- Can the client name someone in her life who could fill that role? If not, she can create a dream mentor as a character in her story.

Crossing the Threshold

At this point in the client's story, we can examine her hero's relationship with vulnerability.

- Why does she do what she does?

- What could her catchphrase be? The answer to this question gives both the coach and the client insight into her current mindset.

- What are some of the hero's deepest fears?
- What negative self-talk does the hero engage in?

Tests, Allies, Enemies

It is important for our clients to consider the broader implications and consequences of her journey. By thinking ahead, she can be prepared to navigate the possibly uncharted waters.

- Who, in her story, might be negatively affected by the hero's progress?
- How might they attempt to throw the hero off balance?
- Who are the hero's most loyal companions and what qualities do they possess that support her?
- What challenges might lie ahead and what strengths will help her overcome them?

Approach to the Inmost Cave

At this stage, the client can take the time to summarize the story up to this point. She can consider the ways in which her hero has become more knowledgeable, skilled and wise.

- What new insights has her hero gained so far?
- Envisioning the path forward, what steps need to be taken for the hero to achieve her goals?
- Which limiting beliefs are resurfacing?

- How do they show up in different contextual realms of her life?

- Having previously turned those limiting beliefs into antagonists in the story, what would she say to these characters now?

The Supreme Ordeal

It is time for the client to consider the inner and outer battles her hero needs to fight to progress forward.

- How does the client's current situation represent her hero's 'ordeal'?

- Now that she has a plan envisioned, what inner obstacles might her hero face?

- In what ways has the hero sabotaged her own progress in the past?

- Who has blocked her momentum in the past?

- Who are the stakeholders that might be affected by the hero's success?

- How will life be different when the hero reaches her goal?

- What inner transformation has she experienced thus far?

The Reward

Here, the client can reflect on any shift in perspective her hero has had along the journey and prepare for the next chapter in her life.

- What new insights, awareness and knowledge has her protagonist gained?

- How might these insights shape the next chapter of the

story?

- What will the theme and title be?
- How has the hero's world view changed?
- What new behaviors has she cultivated?
- What possibilities does she see now that she was unable to envision in the past?
- What potential challenges can she foresee as the hero pre-pares to return to her "ordinary life"?
- And what might she need to leave behind, now that she has achieved the changes she was looking for?

The Return with the Elixir

When the client has accomplished her original goals, she will need to consider the impact the change will have on her ordin-ary life and those around her. Her

transformation may bring with it a new inner strength, new opportunities, new friends and even a possible shift in values. It is helpful to consider these implications and to prepare for them in advance.

- What impact might the hero's transformation have on her loved ones?
- What new opportunities has the transformation brought into the hero's life?
- How might the hero's life be altered?
- To set an intention for the future, what could be the title and theme of the next chapter?

Afterall, more adventures always await us!

Bio

Michelle Hefner is an ICF certified catalyst coach, author and the founder of Zen H Coaching. She partners with clients to discover their dreams and transform them into reality. Whether it's writing a book, starting a business or redesigning their lives, she holds the space for clients to find courage, confidence and comfort in the unknown. She shares a powerful lesson she learned after a fall from her horse, that only through embracing the unknown and learning to thrive in vulnerability can one discover possibilities.

As a certified equine assisted coach, as well, she has engaged teams and leaders in experiential interactions with her horses. Horse wisdom teaches teams to embody the true meaning of alignment, cohesion, clarity of intention and energetic connection. Groups from organizations such as Apple, A Glimmer of Hope, Whole Foods and more have all had the chance to work with her herd.

She lives outside of Austin with her husband, horses, dogs and a cat. They have an Airbnb/retreat cottage where guests can rest, write and experience equine assisted coaching. On the weekends, she is usually riding one of her horses or helping equestrians deepen the bonds of trust with their horses through her 2 day workshop called, Equinelightenment, Discover the Buddha in your Barn.

To learn more, visit zenhcoaching.com.

ACKNOWLEDGEMENT

The idea for this book came to me early one winter morning. I had been pondering how the Austin community of professional coaches could celebrate its 25th anniversary as a united entity. What made it such a privilege to be a part of this group? From the first meeting I attended, the friendly atmosphere made me feel included as a member of the family, a member of the tribe. Over time, the shared values we held as coaches became evident. We each have a passion for our work. We value learning. We are committed to giving back to our profession and to our larger community through volunteer work. It is a group that has a foundational culture of support, connection and collaboration. This book and the process of bringing it to life, exemplifies the spirit of that culture and its values.

I owe many debts of gratitude to all of the authors who pitched in to complete this project.. To Sherry Lowry for her absolute support and continuous encouragement throughout the year and for sharing her vast wisdom in both the introduction and in her chapter. To Elly van Laar for her brilliant idea of hosting weekly Zoom writers' circles that kept the focus alive. To Kandice Klumb for generating a list of wonderful title ideas. To Shelley Pernot for writing the back cover summary and for working with Susan Corbin to research the copyright. To Edna Harris for her "eagle eye" and labor of love in editing the final draft.

Thank you to each of the authors who so generously contributed their time, knowledge and experience to this book. You all enthusiastically embraced my simple idea of capturing our group's collective knowledge, and kept me on track to transform it into a cohesive reality. Ted Middleberg, you amazed me by committing to your chapter and completing it, while traveling the world. This book would not fully represent our community without the voice of Kelley Russell-Duvarney who partnered with Marilynn Orr to contribute a chapter during a challenging summer. Thank you to the rest of our contributors- Michelle Lopez, Teresa Bitner, Diane Dean, Joshua Boyer and Marilnn Orr for all of your powerful insights and your selfless willingness to share.

This collaboration is a true reflection of our community writ large and it has been an honor being a part of it. Here's to our next 25 years.
--Michelle Hefner

Made in the USA
Coppell, TX
15 February 2023

12866872R00115